IP PHRASEBOOKS

HEBREW PHRASEBOOK & SELF STUDY GUIDE

DR. ISRAEL PALCHAN

IP pharesebooks for english speakers

IP

ISBN 9798714765551

e-mail: israel_palchan@yahoo.com

How to use IP Phrasebooks

looking for:

"Please give me a ticket to Jerusalem"

look for:	index: p. 231	page:	find:	
1 please please	▪ p	 22	please 22, 79, 219 bevakasha	 בבקשה
2 give give me	▪ g	 125	give 125 ten li	 תן לי
3 ticket a ticket	▪ t	 94	ticket 94 kartis	 כרטיס
4 to to	▪ t	 21	to 21, 76... 187 le, la	 ל...
5 Jerusalem to Jerusalem	▪ j	 187	Jerusalem 47, 187 leyerushalaim	 לירושלים

result:

"bevakasha ten li kartis leyerushalayim"

בבקשה תן לי כרטיס לירושלים

CONTENT

This book has been produced for tourists and for Hebrew students. The entries in this book are given in three forms: Hebrew, Hebrew transliteration, and English.

The rules for reading the Hebrew and transliteration are explained in the following pages.

The book opens with entries especially useful for the tourist; the subjects include: hotels, transportation, foreign exchange, shopping, law, and health.

The most important thing for a person who is surrounded by people speaking a foreign language to do, is to be able **to ask questions**. If those around him understand him, they will be able to get the answer across, one way or another. Therefore approximately one-third of the book deals with **questions often asked and usual replies**.

The second part of the book contains about **75 useful** verbs including all tenses. It consists of verb declensions: the past and future are presented in two parallel columns, with the present tense above. Verb forms in the present don't change in Hebrew according to pronouns.

The different subjects which cover man's functioning in daily life are found in these two parts of the book according to the appropriate questions and verb.

The third part of the book includes approximately 1,000 expressions commonly found in spoken Hebrew with their English/American equivalents.

The book is constructed in the form of a "language tree"

in a Lego-type system so that the reader can piece together as many sentences as his heart desires and with the examples brought in the book.

At the back of the book is the ***Index*** – a list of words with the number of the pages they appear on, arranged according to the English alphabet. In addition to all the phrases already prepared, you can build sentences on your own using the index. For example, the sentence "***Please help me find this address***". To begin assembling this sentence the reader must search for the first word – "***please***" under the letter "***p***" in the index, and is directed to the page 79 in the book.

On the contents page, you can locate the verb "help," and then go to the page that it is on (page 132) and see the verb diversion and attached phrases. After revealing the phrase "***help me, please***" you can easily find the uncovering rest of the sentence "***...find the place***" as it is on the same page. If you want to change what you are looking for in that sentence, you can use the index in order to replace the word "***place***" with "***address***" and "***the***" with "***this***" from page 24. Finally, the sentence is complete and ready to be said

"***please help me find this address***" –

– "בבקשה תעזור לי למצוא את הכתובת הזאת"

"bevakasha taazor li limtso et haktovet hazot" .

■ How To Read Hebrew

Hebrew is written and read from right to left.

The Alphabet

pronunciation	name of letter	letter	pronunciation	name of letter	letter
l	lamed	ל	—	aleph	א
m	mem	מ, ם*	b,v	beit	ב
n	nun	נ, ן*	g	gimel	ג
s	samekh	ס	d	dalet	ד
—	ain	ע	h	hey	ה
p, f	pey	פ, ף*	v, u, o	vav	ו
ts	tsadi	צ, ץ*	z	zain	ז
k	kuf	ק	kh	khet	ח
r	resh	ר	t	tet	ט
sh	shin	שׁ	y, yi	yod	י
s	sin	שׂ	k, kh	kaf	כ, ך*
t	tav	ת			

*way of writing the letter when it comes at the end of a word.

The letters ב, כ, פ are always pronounced respectively: "*b*", "*k*", "*p*" at the beginning of a word. At the end of a word they are always pronounced "*v*", "*kh*", and "*f*".

The vowel sounds "*a*", "*e*", "*i*", "*o*", "*u*" are not represented in Hebrew by letters. They are represented by "diacritical marks" around the constants and often do not appear in the text.

Here is a list of vowels in Hebrew:

	Name		Name	Sound
אָ	kam*a*tz gad*o*l	אַ	pat*a*kh	a
אֵ	tzeir*e*	אֶ	seg*o*l	e
אִ	khir*i*k gad*o*l	אִ	khir*i*k	i
אוֹ	khol*a*m	אָ	kam*a*ts kat*a*n	o
אוּ	shur*u*k	אֻ	kub*u*ts	oo

"**kamats katan**" appears in a very limited number of words and the reader may pronounce the vowel as "*a*" except in the common word כל – kol – *all*.

Pronunciation Rules

Transliteration	Pronunciation	As in
a	[a]	t**a**r
ay	[ai]	h**igh**
e	[ə]	p**e**t
ey	[əi]	th**ey**
i	[i]	m**ee**t
o	[ɔ]	d**oo**r
u	[oo]	b**oo**t
h	[h]	**h**elp
kh	[kh]	Ba**ch**
tz	[ts]	bi**ts**
z	[z]	chee**s**e
"	signifies a slight pause after the letter as if two words are stuck together	**mar"kiv** = **mar + kiv** **lif"ol=lif+ol**

BASIC GRAMMATICAL STRUCTURES

Masculine and Feminine differ in the suffixes added onto the verbs, nouns and pronouns.

Singular	Masculine		Feminine		
Verb Present	*kotev*	כותב	*kotevet*	**כותבת**	write
Noun	*katav*	כתב	*katevet*	**כתבת**	journalist
Adjective	*katuv*	כתוב	*ktuva*	כתובה	written
Verb past	*katav*	כתב	*katva*	כתבה	wrote

Suffixes used for feminine singular: "**ת**" – "**et**" , "**ה**" – "**a**".
For masculine plural the suffix "**ים**" – "**im**" is added.
For feminine plural the suffix "**ות**" – "**ot**" is added.

For example:

Plural	Masculine		Feminine		English
Verb	*kotvim*	כותבים	*kotvot*	כותבות	are writing
Noun	*katavim*	כתבים	*katavot*	כתבות	journalist
Adjective	*ktuvim*	כתובים	*ktuvot*	כתובות	are written

Unlike in English, in Hebrew it is customary to place the adjective after the noun it describes.

big city	*ir gdola*	עיר **גדולה**
first meeting	*pgisha rishona*	פגישה **ראשונה**

Punctuation Marks

... (ellipsis) – set of three dots, used frequently, indicating continuation of sentence, for example

when...?	*matay...?*	?...מתי
are you free	*ata panuy*	אתה פנוי
can I come over	*ani yakhol lavo*	אני יכול לבוא
to your place	*elekha*	אליך

In other cases, the ellipsis marks the joining of the conjunction and the following into one word

on the...	*ba...*	...ב
ship	*sfina*	ספינה
road	*kvish*	כביש

Comma "," – used frequently to separate the masculine and feminine gender in the Hebrew and transliteration columns

good	*tov, tova*	טוב, טובה
bad	*ra, raa*	רע, רעה
tall	*gavoa, gvoha*	גבוה, גבוהה

(m.) – masculine
(f.) – feminine
(s) – sinqular
(pl) – plural

■ **GREETINGS**

Hello! Hi!	shalom	שלום, בוקר טוב,
Good bye!	shalom, lehitraot	שלום; להתראות
Good morning.	boker tov	בוקר טוב.
Good afternoon.	tsohoraim tovim	צהריים טובים
Good evening.	erev tov	ערב טוב.
Good night!	laila tov	לילה טוב!
See you later!	lehitraot	להתראות!
Yes.	ken	כן.
No.	lo	לא.
Thank you!	toda	תודה
Thank you very much!	toda raba	תודה רבה!
You're welcome!	al lo davar	על לא דבר!
Please give me...	bevaksha ten li	בבקשה תן לי
the ticket.	et hakartis	את הכרטיס.
my passport.	et hadarkon sheli	את הדרכון שלי.
Sorry!	slikha	סליחה!
Excuse me please.	slakh li bevakasha	סלח לי בבקשה.
How are you?	eykh ata margish	איך אתה מרגיש?
OK	beseder	בסדר
Sit down! Sit!	shev	שב!
I don't know.	ani lo yodea	אני לא יודע.
I don't speak English.	ani lo medaber(et) anglit	אני לא מדבר(ת) אנגלית.
Do you speak Hebrew?	ata medaber ivrit?	אתה מדבר עברית?
My name is...	shmi	שמי...
Moshe	Moshe	משה

■ HEALTH

I need a/an...	ani tsarikh...	אני צריך...
doctor	rofe	רופא
hospital	beit kholim	בית חולים
emergency room	khadar miyun	חדר מיון
ambulance	magen david adom	מגן דוד אדום
nurse	akhot	אחות
medicine	trufa	תרופה
I feel a...storm comming	ani margish... keev	אני מרגיש...כאב
I have a/an...	yesh li...	יש לי...
ear, ears	ozen, oznaim	אוזן, אוזניים
eye, eyes	ain, eynaim	עין, עיניים
hand, hand	yad, yadaim	יד, ידים
head	rosh	ראש
heart	lev	לב
leg, legs	regel, regel	רגל, רגלים
problem with...	baaya im...	בעיה עם...
stomach	beten	בטן
(high) temperature	khom	חום
wound	petsa	פצע
I have...	yesh li...	יש לי...
skin	or	עור
hair	saarot	שערות
nails	tsipornaim	ציפורניים
He, she was...	hu haya, hi hayta...	הוא היה, היא היתה...
unconscious	lelo hakara	ללא הכרה
wounded	patsua, ptsua	פצוע, פצועה

in a road accident	*beteunat drakhim*	בתאונת דרכים
I have to...	*ani hayav...*	**...אני חייב**
contact	*lehitkasher*	להתקשר
call	*likro le...*	...לקרוא ל
phone	*letsaltsel*	לצלצל
enter	*lehikanes*	להיכנס
come	*lavo*	לבוא
This must...	*ze tsarikh*	**...זה צריך**
be right	*lihyot nakhon*	להיות נכון

■ POLICE, LAW

I am looking for a/an...	*ani mekhapes...*	**...אני מחפש**
officer	*katsin*	קצין
lawyer	*orekh din*	עורך דין
police department	*mishtara*	משטרה
this is...	*ze...*	**...זה**
an arrest	*maasar*	מאסר
without any reason	*lelo siba*	ללא סיבה
on accusation of...	*beashma*	באשמה
in suspicion of...	*bekhashad shel...*	...בחשד של
theft	*gneva*	גניבה
murder	*retsakh*	רצח
law	*khok*	חוק
prison	*beit kele*	בית כלא
You must...	*ata tsarikh*	**...אתה צריך**
get in touch	*lifnot*	לפנות
call...	*likro le...*	...לקרוא ל
demand	*lidrosh*	לדרוש

contact	*lehitkasher*	להתקשר
know	*ladaat*	לדעת
suspect	*lakhshod*	לחשוד

■ SHOPPING

rate	*taarif*	תעריף
shop	*khanut*	חנות
sale	*mkhira*	מכירה
salesman	*mokher*	מוכר
saleswoman	*mokheret*	מוכרת
price	*mkhir*	מחיר
discount	*hanakha*	הנחה
sale, discount	*mivtsa*	מבצע
gifts/presents	*matanot*	מתנות
souvenir store	*khanut mazkerot*	חנות מזכרות
jewelry store	*khanut takhshitim*	חנות תכשיטים
Supermarket	*supermarket*	סופרמרקט
Supersal (name of supermarket)	*supersal*	שופרסל
Shekem (name of store)	*shekem*	שקם
book store	*khanut sfarim*	חנות ספרים
book (books)	*sefer (sfarim)*	ספר (ספרים)
newspaper (newspapers)	*iton (itonim)*	עיתון (עיתונים)
market	*shuk*	שוק
clothes	*bgadim*	**בגדים**
men's clothing	*bigdey gvarim*	בגדי גברים

women's clothing	bigd**ey** nashim	בגדי נשים
bathing suit	b**eged yam**	בגד ים
cosmetics	tamruk**im**	תמרוקים
camera	matslem**a**	מצלמה
film	s**eret**	סרט
photo	tats**lum**	תצלום
food	maz**on**	מזון
hat	k**ova**	כובע
sandals	sandalim	סנדלים
shorts	shortim	שורטים
souvenirs	mazker**ot**	מזכרות
ticket...	kart**is...**	**כרטיס...**
for the bus	leotobus	לאוטובוס
for the movie	las**eret**	לסרט
for the show	lahatsag**a**	להצגה
trip, hike, sightseeing...	*tiyul...*	**טיול...**
in Jerusalem	birushal**aim**	בירושלים
in the Galilee	bagal**il**	בגליל
in Jordan	beyarden	בירדן
in Egypt	bemitsraim	במצרים
May I to...?	efshar...	**אפשר...?**
buy	likn**ot**	לקנות
choose	livkh**or**	לבחור
drink	lishtot	לשתות
eat	leekh**ol**	לאכול
pay	leshal**em**	לשלם
prefer	lehaad**if**	להעדיף
spend time	leval**ot**	לבלות

■ PREPOSITIONS

above	*meal, meal le...*	מעל, מעל ל...
after...	*akhar...*	אחר...
after that	*akhar kakh*	אחר כך
after	*akharey*	אחרי
after...	*kaavor...*	כעבור...
against	*neged*	נגד
around...	*saviv, saviv le...*	סביב, סביב ל...
all around	*misaviv*	מסביב
as compared to...	*behashvaa le...*	בהשוואה ל...
as opposed to...	*leumat...*	לעומת...
at	*etsel*	אצל
because of	*biglal*	בגלל
between	*beyn*	בין
by	*al yedey*	על ידי
except for...	*khuts mi...*	חוץ מ...
for	*bead, bishvil*	בעד, בשביל
for	*lemaan*	למען
from...	*min, me...*	מן, מ...
from under...	*mitakhat le...*	מתחת ל...
in...	*be...*	ב...
inside	*bifnim, betokh*	בפנים, בתוך
instead of	*bimkom*	במקום
into	*letokh*	לתוך
like	*kmo*	כמו
next to	*al yad*	על יד
not	*bilti, lo*	בלתי, לא
on	*al*	על

on the contrary	*leheyfekh*	להיפך
opposite	*mul*	מול
through...	*bead...*	בעד...
through...	*derekh...*	דרך...
to...	*el, le...*	אל, ל...
towards	*likrat*	לקראת
until	*ad*	עד
while	*beod*	בעוד
with	*im*	עם
with the help of	*beezrat*	בעזרת
without	*bli*	בלי

■ WH – QUESTIONS

who?	*mi?*	מי?
what?	*ma?*	מה?
where?	*eyfo?*	איפה?
where to?	*lean?*	לאן?
where to?	*leeyfo?*	לאיפה?
where from?	*meeyfo?*	מאיפה?
when?	*matay?*	מתי?
which (m.)	*eyze?*	איזה?
which (f.)	*eyzo?*	איזו?
why?	*lama?*	למה?
why?	*madua?*	מדוע?
why not?	*lama lo?*	למה לא?
how?	*eykh?*	איך?
how much? (many)	*kama?*	כמה?

■ Conjunctions

also, too	gam, gam ken	גם, גם כן
and...	ve...	ו...
because	keyvan she	כיוון ש...
but	aval	אבל
despite...	af al pi she...	אף על פי ש...
even	afilu	אפילו
even more so	al akhat kama vekhama	על אחת כמה וכמה
if	im	אם
if	lu, ilu	לו, אילו
moreover	yeter al ken	יתר על כן
or	o	או
that	asher (she...)	אשר, ש...
that means	zot omeret	זאת אומרת
unless	ilmale	אלמלא
when	kaasher (kshe...)	כאשר, כש...

■ Exclamation Words

God forbid!	khalila	חלילה
God forbid!	khas vekhalila	חס וחלילה
Oh my God!	oy vaavoy li	אוי ואבוי לי
come on, lets	hava	הבה
I wish	halevay	הלוואי
of course	vaday, bevaday	וודאי, בודאי
perfect	metsuyan	מצוין
it's a pity (that...)	khaval she...	חבל ש...
please	bevakasha	בבקשה

Quiet!	*sheket*	!שקט
Really?!	*bekhayekha?!*	!?בחייך
Really!, Sure!	*bekhayay!*	!בחיי
well	*tov*	טוב
very well	*tov meod*	טוב מאוד
without a doubt	*bli safek*	בלי ספק
wonderful, great	*nehedar, yofi*	נהדר, יופי

■ PRONOUNS
PERSONAL PRONOUNS

I	*ani*	אני
you (m.)	*ata*	אתה
you (f.)	*at*	את
he	*hu*	הוא
she	*hi*	היא
we	*anakhnu*	
you (m.pl.)	*atem*	אתם
you (f.pl.)	*aten*	אתן
they (m.)	*hem*	הם
they (f.)	*hen*	הן
me	*oti*	אותי
you (m.)	*otkha*	אותך
you (f.)	*otakh*	אותך
him, it	*oto*	אותו
her	*ota*	אותה
us	*otanu*	אותנו
you (m.pl.)	*etkhem*	אתכם
you (f.pl.)	*etkhen*	אתכן
them (m.)	*otam*	אותם

them (f.)	otan	אותן
to me	li	לי
to you (m.)	lekha	לך
to you (f.)	lakh	לך
to him, to it	lo	לו
to her	la	לה
to us	lanu	לנו
to you (m.pl.)	lakhem	לכם
to you (f.pl.)	lakhen	לכן
to them (m.)	lahem	להם
to them (f.)	lahen	להן

POSSESSIVE PRONOUNS

of (somebodys)	shel	של...
my, mine	sheli	שלי
your, yours (m.)	shelkha	שלך
your, yours (f.)	shelakh	שלך
his	shelo	שלו
her, hers	shela	שלה
our, ours	shelanu	שלנו
your, yours (m.pl.)	shelakhem	שלכם
your, yours (f.pl.)	shelakhen	שלכן
their, theirs (m.)	shelahem	שלהם
their, theirs (f.)	shelahen	שלהן

DEMONSTRATIVE PRONOUNS

| this (m.) | ze | זה |
| this (f.) | zot, zo | זאת, זו |

| these (m., f.) | **ey**le, **ey**lu | אילה, אילו |

Reflexive Pronouns

for/to myself	leatsmi	לעצמי
for/to yourself (m.)	leatsmekha	לעצמך
for/to yourself (f.)	leatsmekh	לעצמך
for/to himself	leatsmo	לעצמו
for/to herself	leatsma	לעצמה
for/to ourselves	leatsmeynu	לעצמינו
for/to yourselves (m.pl.)	leatsmekhem	לעצמכם
for/to yourselves (f.pl.)	leatsmekhen	לעצמכן
to themselves	leatsmam (-n')	לעצמם, לעצמן
there is/are	yesh	יש
there is/are not	eyn	אין
here is	hine	הנה

■ Adverbs

Adverbs of Place

above	lemala	למעלה
from above	milemala	מלמעלה
around	saviv	סביב
backwards	akhora, leakhor	אחורה, לאחור
below	lemata	למטה
from below	milemata	מלמטה
further	hala	הלאה
forward	kadima	קדימה
from a distance	merakhok	מרחוק
from where?	meayin	מאין

here (to this place)	*hena*	הנה
here	*po, kan*	פה, כאן
there (to that place)	*lesham*	לשם
there	*sham*	שם
where	**ey**fo, heykhan*	איפה, היכן
where to?	*lean*	לאן

ADVERBS OF TIME

afterwards	*akharkakh*	אחר כך
already	*kvar*	כבר
always	*tamid*	תמיד
early	*mukdam*	מוקדם
finally	*sof sof*	סוף סוף
first	*kodem*	קודם
first of all	*tkhila*	תחילה
forever	*leolam, letamid*	לעולם, לתמיד
immediately	*miyad*	מיד
in the end	*besofo shel davar*	בסופו של דבר
late	*meukhar*	מאוחר
long ago	*mizman*	מזמן
meanwhile	*beintaim*	בינתיים
never	*af paam*	אף פעם
now	*akhshav*	עכשיו
often	*leitim krovot*	לעיתים קרובות
rarely	*leitim rekhokot*	לעיתים רחוקות
recently	*lo mizman*	לא מזמן
since, from then	*meaz*	מאז
since when?	*mimatay*	?ממתי

sometimes	*lifamim, leitim*	לפעמים, לעיתים
soon	*bekarov*	בקרוב
still, more	*od*	עוד
still, yet	*od, adain*	עוד, עדיין
suddenly	*pitom, lefeta*	פתאום, לפתע
then	*az*	אז
until when?	*ad matay*	עד מתי?
urgent	*dakhuf*	דחוף
when?	*matay*	מתי?

General Adverbs & Conjunctions

according to	*lefi, kfi,*	לפי, כפי,
	behet"em le...	בהתאם ל...
after all	*akhrey hakol*	אחרי הכול
again	*shuv*	שוב
alone	*levad*	לבד
altogether	*bikhlal*	בכלל
bad	*ra*	רע
because...	*mipney she...*	מפני ש...
behold	*harey, sim lev*	הרי, שים לב!
certainly, for sure	*kamuvan, betakh*	כמובן, בטח
certainly	*bevaday*	בוודאי
clearly	*barur*	ברור
correct, right	*nakhon*	נכון
could be	*yakhol lihyot*	יכול להיות
despite...	*af al pi she...,*	אף על פי ש....,
	lamrot	למרות
do you?	*haim*	האם?

enough	*maspik*	מספיק
entirely	*legamrey*	לגמרי
clear, evident	*muvan meelav*	מובן מאליו
exactly	*bediyuk*	בדיוק
not exactly	*lo bediyuk*	לא בדיוק
few, a few	*meat*	מעט
for nothing	*lashav*	לשוא
free	*khinam, bekhinam*	חינם, בחינם
good	*tov*	טוב
hastily	*bakhipazon*	בחיפזון
in order	*kdey*	כדי
incorrect, wrong	*lo nakhon*	לא נכון
it is not possible	*lo yitakhen*	לא יתכן
it is possible	*yitakhen*	יתכן
just, only	*stam*	סתם, רק
less	*pakhot*	פחות
like	*kmo (ki, ke...)*	כמו, כ...
little, a little	*ktsat*	קצת
much	*harbe*	הרבה
more	*yoter*	יותר
the most	*hakhi*	הכי
many	*rabim*	רבים
no, not	*lo*	לא
not quite	*lo bid"yuk*	לא בדיוק
not so good	*lo kol kakh*	לא כל כך
not so much	*lo kol kakh*	לא כל כך
nothing	*klum, meuma*	כלום, מאומה
once	*paam*	פעם

otherwise	*akheret*	אחרת
perhaps	*ulay*	אולי
possible	*efshar*	אפשר
precisely	*bid"yuk*	בדיוק
quickly	*maher*	מהר
really	*haomnam*	האומנם
seemingly	*kivyakhol*	כביכול
slowly	*leat*	לאט
so beautiful	*kol kakh yafe, yafa*	כל כך יפה
so what?	*az ma*	אז מה
so (like this)	*kakh, kakha*	כך, ככה
so	*kol kakh*	כל כך
some kind of	*mashehu kmo*	משהו כמו
something	*mashehu*	משהו
there is no need	*eyn tsorekh*	אין צורך
there isn't, there is no	*eyn*	אין
therefore	*al ken, lakhen*	על כן, לכן
together	*yakhad*	יחד
totally	*lekhalutin*	לחלוטין
twice	*paamaim*	פעמיים
very	*meod*	מאוד
yes	*ken*	כן

■ NUMBERS

MASCULINE:

one	ekhad	אחד
two	shnaim	שניים
three	shlosha	שלושה
four	arbaa	ארבעה
five	khamisha	חמישה
six	shisha	שישה
seven	shiva	שבעה
eight	shmona	שמונה
nine	tisha	תשעה
ten	asara	עשרה
eleven	akhad asar	אחד עשר
twelve	shneim asar	שנים עשר
thirteen	shlosha asar	שלושה עשר
fourteen	arbaa asar	ארבעה עשר
fifteen	khamisha asar	חמישה עשר
sixteen	shisha asar	שישה עשר
seventeen	shiva asar	שבעה עשר
eighteen	shmona asar	שמונה עשר
nineteen	tisha asar	תשעה עשר

FEMININE:

one	akhat	אחת
two	shtaim	שתיים
three	shalosh	שלוש
four	arba	ארבע
five	khamesh	חמש

six	*shesh*	שש
seven	*sheva*	שבע
eight	*shmone*	שמונה
nine	*teysha*	תשע
ten	*eser*	עשר
eleven	*akhat esre*	אחת עשרה
twelve	*shteyim esre*	שתים עשרה
thirteen	*shlosh esre*	שלוש עשרה
fourteen	*arba esre*	ארבע עשרה
fifteen	*khamesh esre*	חמש עשרה
sixteen	*shesh esre*	שש עשרה
seventeen	*shva esre*	שבע עשרה
eighteen	*shmone esre*	שמונה עשרה
nineteen	*tsha esre*	תשע עשרה
twenty	*esrim*	עשרים
thirty	*shloshim*	שלושים
forty	*arbaim*	ארבעים
fifty	*khamishim*	חמישים
sixty	*shishim*	שישים
seventy	*shivim*	שבעים
eighty	*shmonim*	שמונים
ninety	*tishim*	תשעים
a hundred	*mea*	מאה
two hundred	*mataim*	מאתים
three hundred	*shlosh meot*	שלוש מאות
· · · · · · · · · · ·		
nine hundred	*tsha meot*	תשע מאות
thousand	*elef*	אלף

two thousand	*alpayim*	אלפיים
three thousand	*shloshet alafim*	שלושת אלפים
. . . .	. . . .	. . . .
seven thousand	*shivat alafim*	שבעת אלפים
. . . .	. . . .	. . . .
ten thousand	*aseret alafim*	עשרת אלפים
a million	*milyon*	מיליון

ORDINAL NUMBERS (M.)

first	*rishon*	ראשון
second	*sheni*	שני
third	*shlishi*	שלישי
fourth	*revii*	רביעי
fifth	*khamishi*	חמישי
sixth	*shishi*	שישי
seventh	*shvii*	שביעי
eighth	*shmini*	שמיני
ninth	*tshii*	תשיעי
tenth	*asiri*	עשירי

ORDINAL NUMBERS (F.)

first	*rishona*	ראשונה
second	*shniya*	שניה
third	*shlishit*	שלישית
fourth	*reviit*	רביעית
fifth	*khamishit*	חמישית
sixth	*shishit*	שישית
seventh	*shviit*	שביעית

eighth	*shminit*	שמינית
ninth	*tshiit*	תשיעית
tenth	*asirit*	עשירית

FRACTIONS

half	*khetsi, makhatsit*	חצי, מחצית
third	*shlish*	שליש
two-thirds	*shney shlish*	שני שליש
quarter	*reva*	רבע
fifth	*khamishit*	חמישית
sixth	*shishit*	שישית
seventh	*shviit*	שביעית
eighth	*shminit*	שמינית
ninth	*tshiit*	תשיעית
tenth	*asirit*	עשירית
hundredth	*meit*	מאית
thousandth	*alpit*	אלפית
fifteenth	*khelek hakhamisha asar*	חלק החמישה עשר
three fifteenths	*shlolsha khelkey khamisha asar*	שלושה חלקי חמישה עשר

■ Who...

Who Phrases

Who?	mi?	?מי
Who are you?	mi ata, at?	?מי אתה, את
Who is coming?	mi ba?	?מי בא
Who is giving?	mi noten?	?מי נותן
Who is he, she?	mi hu, hi?	?מי הוא, היא
Who is hungry?	mi raev?	?מי רעב
Who is opposed?	mi mitnaged?	?מי מתנגד
Who is sick?	mi khole?	?מי חולה
Who is talking?	mi medaber?	?מי מדבר
Who is there (here)?	mi ze sham (kan)?	?(מי זה שם (כאן
Who is this?	mi ze?	?מי זה
Who is tired?	mi ayef?	?מי עייף
Who moved?	mi avar?	?מי עבר
Who prefers?	mi maadif?	?מי מעדיף
Who said?	mi amar?	?מי אמר
Who saw?	mi raa?	?מי ראה
Who wants?	mi rotse?	?מי רוצה
Who wants to drink?	mi rotse lishtot?	?מי רוצה לשתות
Who went?	mi halakh?	?מי הלך
Who went out?	mi yatsakh?	?מי יצא
Who's against?	mi neged?	?מי נגד
Who's in favor?	mi bead?	?מי בעד
Who's waiting for you?	mi mekhake lekha, lakh?	מי מחכה ?לך
Who's with us?	mi itanu?	?מי אתנו

Who's with you?	*mi itkha? mi itakh?* (f.)	מי אתך?
whoever...	*mi she...*	**מי ש...**
believes	*maamin,*	מאמין,
	maamina	מאמינה
demands	*doresh, doreshet*	דורש, דורשת
finishes	*gomer, gomeret*	גומר, גומרת
gives	*noten, notenet*	נותן, נותנת
hears	*shomea, shomaat*	שומע, שומעת
knows	*yodea, yodaat*	יודע, יודעת
pays	*meshalem,*	משלם,
	meshalemet	משלמת
sits	*yoshev, yoshevet*	יושב, יושבת
stands	*omed, omedet*	עומד, עומדת
starts	*matkhil, matkhila*	מתחיל, מתחילה
thinks	*khoshev, khoshevet*	חושב, חושבת
thinks, reckons	*savur, svura*	סבור, סבורה
wants	*rotse, rotsa*	רוצה, רוצה
this is a/an...	*ze...*	**זה....**
agent (m.)	*sokhen*	סוכן
agent (f.)	*sokhenet*	סוכנת
army officer	*katsin, ktsina*	קצין, קצינה
clerk, carrier	*pakid, pkida*	פקיד, פקידה
daughter, girl	*bat*	בת
doctor	*rofe, rofa*	רופא, רופאה
driver	*nahag, naheget*	נהג, נהגת
father	*aba*	אבא
a fellow that...	*bakhur she...*	בחור ש...
a girl that...	*bakhura she...*	בחורה ש...

grandfather	*saba*	סבא
grandmother	*savta*	סבתא
guide (m.),	*madrikh,*	מדריך,
(f.)	*madrikha*	מדריכה
mailman	*davar*	דוור
manager	*menahel*	מנהל
mother	*ima*	אמא
nurse	*akhot*	אחות
policeman (m.), (f.)	*shoter, shoteret*	שוטר, שוטרת
porter	*sabal*	סבל
salesman	*mokher*	מוכר
salesperson (m.),	*mokher,*	מוכר,
(f.)	*mokheret*	מוכרת
saleswoman	*mokheret*	מוכרת
soldier (m.), (f.)	*khayal, khayelet*	חייל, חיילת
son	*ben*	בן
technician	*tekhnai*	טכנאי
tourist (m.)	*tayar*	תייר
(f.)	*tayeret*	תיירת
waiter, waitress	*meltsar, meltsarit*	מלצר, מלצרית
This is...	*ze...*	**...זה**
my husband	*baali*	בעלי
my wife	*ishti*	אשתי
my neighbor	*shakhen*	שכן

■ **WHAT...**

KITCHEN UTENSILS. FOOD. THE HUMAN BODY

What?	*ma?*	?מה
From what?	*mima?*	?...ממה ש
What are you (m.) looking at?	*al ma ata mistakel?*	על מה אתה מסתכל?
What are you reading?	*ma ata kore?, at koret?*	,?מה אתה קורא (את קוראת?)
What are you writing?	*ma ata kotev?, at kotevet?*	,?מה אתה כותב את כותבת?
What did you take?	*ma lakakhta?*	?מה לקחת
What do you care?	*ma ikhpat lekha, lakh?*	?מה איכפת לך
What do you feel?	*ma ata margish?, at margisha?*	,?מה אתה מרגיש את מרגישה?
What do you (m.) intend to do?	*ma ata mitkaven laasot?*	מה אתה מתכוון לעשות?
What do you need for...?	*ma ata tsarikh bishvil...?*	מה אתה צריך בשביל...?
What do you see?	*ma ata roe (at roa)?*	מה אתה רואה (את רואה?)
What do you want from me?	*ma ata rotse mimeni?*	מה אתה רוצה ממני?
What happened?	*ma kara?*	?מה קרה
What happened to him, her?	*ma kara lo, la?*	?מה קרה לו, לה
What is this?	*ma ze?*	?מה זה

What is your name (m.)?	*ma shimkha?*	?מה שמך
What is your name (f.)?	*ma shmekh?*	?מה שמך
What time is it?	*ma hashaa?*	?מה השעה
What's happening here?	*ma kore po (kan)?*	מה קורה פה (כאן)?
What's the matter, what is there?	*ma yesh?*	?מה יש
What's this here (there)?	*ma ze kan (sham)?*	מה זה כאן (שם)?
What's this here?	*ma yesh kan (po)?*	?מה יש כאן (פה)
What's going?	*ma hamatsav?*	?מה המצב
What's with you (m.)?	*ma yesh lekha, lakh?*	?מה יש לך
What's with you (m., f.)?	*ma itkha, itakh?*	?מה אתך, אתך
What will be there?	*ma yih"ye sham?*	?מה יהיה שם
that ...	*ma she...*	...מה ש
that is necessary	*ma shetsarikh*	מה שצריך
this is a, an...	*ze*	...זה
chair	*kise*	כסא
cup	*kos*	כוס
dish	*tsalakhat*	צלחת
fork	*mazleg*	מזלג
knife	*sakin*	סכין
mug	*sefel*	ספל
oven	*tanur*	תנור
refrigerator	*mekarer*	מקרר
table	*shulkhan*	שולחן
tablespoon	*kaf*	כף

teaspoon	*kapit*	כפית
here is...	*kan nimtsa*	כאן נמצא...
here are...	*yesh kan...*	**יש כאן...**
apples	*tapukhey ets*	תפוחי עץ
bread	*lekhem*	לחם
butter	*khem"a*	חמאה
cabbage	*kruv*	כרוב
carrot	*gezer*	גזר
cookies	*ugiyot*	עוגיות
cucumbers	*melafefonim*	מלפפונים
fish	*dag*	דג
juice	*mits*	מיץ
meat	*basar*	בשר
milk	*khalav*	חלב
oil	*shemen*	שמן
onion	*batsal*	בצל
oranges	*tapuzim*	תפוזים
plums	*shezifim*	שזיפים
potato	*tapuakh adama*	תפוח אדמה
salt	*melakh*	מלח
sugar	*sukar*	סוכר
tomatoes	*agvaniyot*	עגבניות
water	*maim*	מים
cream cheese	*gvina levana*	גבינה לבנה
yellow cheese	*gvina tsehuba*	גבינה צהובה
what do you feel?	*ma ata margish?, at margisha*	**מה אתה מרגיש?, את מרגישה?**
I'm perfectly fine.	*ani beseder gamur*	אני בסדר גמור/

I don't feel well.	ani lo margish tov	אני לא מרגיש טוב/
my... hurts	koev li...	**כואב לי...**
back	gav	גב
chest	khaze	חזה
ear	ozen	אוזן
eye	ain	עין
foot	regel	רגל
hand	kaf hayad	כף היד
	yad	יד
head	rosh	ראש
heart	lev	לב
knee	berekh	ברך
liver	kaved	כבד
mouth	pe	פה
nose	af	אף
skin	haor	העור
stomach	beten	בטן
teeth	shinaim	שיניים
throat	garon	גרון
tongue	lashon	לשון
It hurts me here.	koev li kan	כואב לי כאן
My teeth hurt.	koavot li hashinaim	כואבת לי השיניים
There is nothing here.	eyn kan shum davar	אין כאן שום דבר
There are many different things here:	yesh kan harbe dvarim shonim...	**יש כאן הרבה דברים שונים:**
armchair	kursa	כורסה

bed	mita	מיטה
book (books)	sefer (sfarim)	ספר (ספרים)
closet	aron	ארון
lamp	menora	מנורה
notebook with	makhberet im	מחברת עם
pencils	efronot	עפרונות
radio	radio	רדיו
rug	shatiyakh	שטיח
I don't need anything.	ani lo tsarikh shum davar	אני לא צריך שום דבר.
Nothing is happening here.	lo kore kan shum davar	לא קורה כאן שום דבר.
All is quiet.	hakol shaket	הכל שקט.
It is written here...	kan katuv	כאן כתוב...
that I am from...	sheani me...	**שאני מ...**
Argentina	argentina	ארגנטינה
Australia	ostraliya	אוסטרליה
Brazil	brazil	ברזיל
Canada	kanada	קנדה
China	sin	סין
England	angliya	אנגליה
France	tsorfat	צרפת
Germania	germaniya	גרמניה
India	hodu	הודו
Italya	italiya	איטליה
Japan	yapan	יפן
Korea	koria	קורייאה
Spain	sfarad	ספרד

United State	*artsot habrit*	ארצות הברית
What are you writing?	*ma ata kotev*	**?מה אתה כותב**
I am writing...	*ani kotev...*	**אני כותב**
	(kotevet)	**(כותבת)...**
a letter	*mikhtav*	מכתב
a newspaper article	*maamar leiton*	מאמר לעיתון
an explanation	*hesber*	הסבר
resume	*korot khaim*	קורות חיים
I am reading...	*ani kore...*	**אני קורא...**
a book	*sefer*	ספר
a text book	*sefer limud*	ספר לימוד
notice	*modaa*	מודעה
classified ads	*modaot*	מודעות
an article	*maamar*	מאמר
newspaper	*iton*	עיתון
explanation sheet	*daf hesber*	דף הסבר
the instructions	*horaot shimush*	הוראות שימוש
questionnaire	*sheelon*	שאלון

■ **WHERE**

DIFFERENT PLACES, DIRECTIONS

where?	**ey**fo	?איפה
Where is...?	**ey**fo ze	**?איפה זה**
the discotheque	diskotek	דיסקוטק
the hotel	mal**on**	מלון
the map	mapa	מפה
the museum	muze**on**	מוזיאון
the pub	pub	פאב
the night club	moad**on** layla	מועדון לילה
the street	rkhov	רחוב
the youth hostel	akhsaniyat n**oar**	אכסניית נוער
Where about is it?	**ey**fo ze kan?	?איפה זה כאן
Where are you (pl.), they?	**ey**fo atem (hem)?	איפה אתם (הם)?
Where are you?	**ey**fo ata, at?	?איפה אתה, את
Where did you (m.) meet her?	**ey**fo nifgashta ita?	איפה נפגשת אתה?
Where did you put it?	**ey**fo samta, samt et ze?	איפה שמת את זה?
Where did you see it?	**ey**fo raita et ze?	איפה ראית את זה?
Where do you want to live? (m.)	**ey**fo ata rotse likhy**ot**?	איפה אתה רוצה לחיות?
Where is he?	**ey**fo hu nimtsa? **ey**fo hu?	?איפה הוא נמצא ?איפה הוא
Where is it happening?	**ey**fo ze mitrakhesh (kore)?	איפה זה מתרחש (קורה)?

Where is it located?	**ey**fo ze nimtsa?	?איפה זה נמצא
Where will it be?	**ey**fo ze yih"ye?	?איפה זה יהיה
Where is...?	**ey**fo...?	**?...איפה**
my father	aba	אבא
my mother	ima	אמא
my brother	akhi	אחי
my children	hayeladim sheli	הילדים שלי
my sister	akhoti	אחותי
Where is there a/an...?	**ey**fo yesh kan...?	**?...איפה יש כאן**
bank	bank	בנק
bus	**o**tobus	אוטובוס
clinic	kupat kholim	קופת חולים
coffee shop	beyt kafe	בית קפה
dentist	rofe shinaim	רופא שיניים
grocery	mak**o**let	מכולת
hotel	mal**o**n	מלון
information center	modiin	מודיעין
kindergarten	gan yeladim	גן ילדים
manager	hamenah**e**l	המנהל
market	shuk	שוק
Where is...?	**ey**fo...?	**?...איפה**
my group	hakvutsa sheli	הקבוצה שלי
nursery	peut**o**n	פעוטון
police station	mishtar**a**	משטרה
post office	had**o**ar	הדואר
reception	hakabal**a**	הקבלה
restaurant	mis"ada	מסעדה
school	beyt sefer	בית ספר

shop	*khanut*	חנות
supermarket	*supermarket*	סופרמרקט
my luggage	*hamizvadot sheli*	המזוודות שלי
Where are...?	***eyfo...?***	**?...איפה**
my friends	*hayedidim*	הידידים
the keys	*hamaftekhot*	המפתחות
there, it's there,	*sham, ze sham,*	,שם, זה שם
here	*kan, po*	כאן, פה
somewhere...	***eyfo shehu...***	**...איפה שהוא**
there	*sham*	שם
after	*akharey*	אחרי
around	*mesaviv*	מסביב
behind	*akharey*	אחרי
straight	*yashar*	ישר
to the left	*smola*	שמאלה
to the right	*yemina*	ימינה
it's in this direction	*ze bekivun haze*	זה בכיוון הזה
It is located...	*ze nimtsa...*	**...זה נמצא**
around the corner	*mesaviv lapina*	מסביב לפינה
in the center of town	*bamerkaz hair*	במרכז העיר
in the closet	*baaron*	בארון
in the handbag	*batik*	בתיק
in the room	*bakheder*	בחדר
in the street	*barkhov*	ברחוב
on the corner	*bapina*	בפינה
in that direction	*bakivun hahu*	בכיוון ההוא
He is...	*hu...*	**...הוא**
in class	*beshiur*	בשיעור

at the clinic	*bekupat kholim*	בקופת חולים
at the hotel	*bamalon*	במלון
at the office	*bamisrad*	במשרד
at the store	*bakhanut*	בחנות
at work	*baavoda*	בעבודה
in his room	*bakheder shelo*	בחדר שלו
in the bathroom	*beambatiya*	באמבטיה
in the kitchen	*bamitbakh*	במטבח
in the toilet	*besherutim*	בשירותים
on a bus	*beotobus*	באוטובוס
on a trip	*betiyul*	בטיול
I put it...	*ani samti et ze...*	**....אני שמתי את זה**
in the closet	*betokh haaron*	בתוך הארון
in the corner	*bapina*	בפינה
in the handbag	*batik*	בטיק
on the chair	*al hakise*	על הכיסא
on the table	*al hashulkhan*	על השולחן
on the television	*al hateleviziya*	על הטלוויזיה
under the table	*mitakhat*	מתחת
	lashulkhan	לשולחן
I saw it...	*raiti et ze...*	**....ראיתי את זה**
close	*karov*	קרוב
far	*rakhok*	רחוק
straight down	*yashar berkhov*	ישר ברחוב
this street	*haze*	הזה
two bus stops	*shtey takhanot*	שתי תחנות
from here	*otobus mikan*	אוטובוס מכאן
in that building	*babinyan hahu*	בבניין ההוא

I don't know, ask someone else.	*lo yodea, tish"al mishehu akher*	לא יודע, תשאל מישהו אחר.
I want to live...	*ani rotse (rotsa f.) likhyot*	**אני רוצה לחיות...**
in the ... hotel	*bemalon...*	במלון...
expensive/dear	*yakar*	יקר
reasonably priced	*bemkhir beynoni*	במחיר בינוני
cheap	*zol*	זול
in the center of the country	*bemerkaz haarets*	במרכז הארץ
in Jerusalem	*birushlaim*	בירושלים
I want to visit...	*ani rotse levaker...*	**אני רוצה לבקר...**
Old City	*hair haatika*	העיר העתיקה
Church of the Holy Sepulchre	*knesiyat hakever*	כנסיית הקבר
Jerusalem	*be Yerushalaim*	בירושלים
the North	*batsafon*	בצפון
the Galilee	*bagalil*	בגליל
the South	*badarom*	בדרום
the Negev	*banegev*	בנגב
the Dead Sea	*beyam hamelakh*	בים המלח
Eilat	*beeylat*	באילת
(to) where	*leeyfo, lean*	לאיפה, לאן
Where are you going? (m.) (f.)	*lean ata holekh?, at holekhet?*	לאן אתה הולך?, את הולכת?
Where did he go?	*lean hu halakh?*	לאן הוא הלך?
Where do you need to go? (m.)	*lean ata tsarikh?*	לאן אתה צריך?

Where do you plan to go?	*lean ata mitkaven lalekhet?*	לאן אתה מתכוון ללכת?
Where is this bus going?	*lean nosea haotobus haze?*	לאן נוסע האוטובוס הזה?
Where did he disappear to?	*lean hu neelam?*	לאן הוא נעלם?
there	*lesham*	לשם
to...	*le...*	...ל
up	*lemala*	למעלה
down	*lemata*	למטה
to the...	*la...*	...ל
bank	*bank*	בנק
bus	*otobus*	אוטובוס
center	*merkaz*	מרכז
clinic	*kupat kholim*	קופת חולים
dentist	*rofe shinaim*	רופא שיניים
doctor	*rofe*	רופא
hospital	*beyt kholim*	בית חולים
hotel	*malon*	מלון
Jewish Agency	*sokhnut*	סוכנות
movie, movies	*seret, kolnoa*	סרט, קולנוע
office	*misrad*	משרד
post office	*doar*	דואר
relatives	*krovim*	קרובים
restaurant	*mis"ada*	מסעדה
beach	*yam*	ים
toilet	*sherutim*	שרותים
work	*avoda*	עבודה

to town	*haira, lair*	העירה, לעיר
on a trip	*latiyul*	לטיול
abroad	*lekhuts laarets*	לחוץ לארץ
shopping	*lakniyot*	לקניות

■ WHERE ...FROM?

Where... from?	*meeyfo, meayin?*	?מאיפה, מאין
Where are you from? (m.)	*meeyfo ata?*	?מאיפה אתה
Where are you from? (f.)	*meeyfo at?*	?מאיפה את
Where is this from?	*meeyfo ze?*	?מאיפה זה
Where do (did) you come from? (m.)	*meeyfo ata?*	?מאיפה אתה
Where did you from?, Where are you from?	*meeyfo at?*	**?מאיפה את**
know	*yodea, yodaat*	יודע, יודעת
come	*ba, baa*	בא, באה
travel	*nosea, nosaat*	נוסע, נוסעת
go	*holekh, holekhet*	הולך, הולכת
take this (m.)	*lakakhta et ze*	לקחת את זה
hear this (m.)	*shamata et ze*	שמעת את זה
What is this based on?	*meeyfo ze novea?*	?מאיפה זה נובע
Where... from?	*meeyfo...?*	**?...מאיפה**
are these rumors	*hashmuot haele*	השמועות האלה
is this information	*hayediot haele*	הידיעות האלה
is this news	*hakhadashot haele*	החדשות האלה
are these fears	*hapekhadim haele*	הפחדים האלה

from there	*misham*	משם
from here	*mikan*	מכאן
from...	*mi...*	**...מ**
New York	*nyu york*	ניו יורק
California	*kalifornia*	קליפורניה
a bank	*bank*	בנק
a clerk	*pakid*	פקיד
a hotel	*malon*	מלון
a store	*khanut*	חנות
a teacher	*more*	מורה
from me	*mimeni*	ממני
from you (m.)	*mimkha*	ממך
from you (f.)	*mimekh*	ממך
from him	*mimenu*	ממנו
from her	*mimena*	ממנה
from us	*mimenu, meitanu*	ממנו, מאיתנו
from you (pl.)	*mikem*	מכם
from them	*mihem*	מהם
from all this	*mikol ze*	מכל זה

■ WHEN...

TIME

When?	*matay?*	?מתי
When did this happen?	*matay ze kara?*	?מתי זה קרה
When will arrive, take place?	*matay ze yih"ye?*	?מתי זה יהיה
When will there be...?	*matay yih"ye...?*	**?...מתי יהיה**
a match	*miskhak*	משחק

a lesson	*shiur*	שיעור
a trip	*tiyul*	טיול
a TV broadcast	*shidur televiziya*	שידור טלוויזיה
There will be...	*tih"ye...*	**תהיה...**
a break, an intermission	*hafsaka*	הפסקה
breakfast	*arukhat boker*	ארוחת בוקר
concert	*kontsert*	קונצרט
dinner	*arukhat erev*	ארוחת ערב
lunch	*arukhat tsohoraim*	ארוחת צהריים
the meeting	*pgisha*	פגישה
the play	*hatsaga*	הצגה
the paid	*maskoret*	משכורת
a trip	*nesia*	נסיעה
When will you be back?	*matay ata khozer?, at khozeret?*	?מתי אתה חוזר, את חוזרת?
When are you (pl.) coming?	*matay atem baim (tavou)?*	מתי אתם באים (תבואו)?
When did he go?	*matay hu halakh?*	**מתי הוא הלך?**
to see a doctor	*lerofe*	לרופא
to school	*labeyt hasefer*	לבית הספר
to class	*lashiur*	לשיעור
to the office	*lamisrad*	למשרד
to the beach	*layam*	לים
to the store	*lakhanut*	לחנות
When will you get it?	*matay tekabel et ze, zot*	מתי תקבל את זה, זאת?

When do you want to do it?	*matay ata rotse laasot et ze?*	מתי אתה רוצה לעשות את זה?
When will you have time?	*matay yesh lekha zman?*	מתי יש לך זמן?
When are going to meet?	*matay anakhnu nifgashim?*	מתי אנחנו נפגשים?
When is it over?	*matay ze nigmar?*	**מתי זה נגמר?**
next week	*beshavua haba*	בשבוע הבא
on Friday evening	*beerev shabat*	בערב שבת
on Saturday evening	*bemotsey shabat*	במוצאי שבת
When...?	*matay...?*	**מתי...?**
are you free	*ata panuy*	אתה פנוי
can I come over to you place	*ani yakhol lavo elekha*	אני יכול לבוא אליך
can we meet	*anakhnu yekholim lehipagesh*	אנחנו יכולים להפגש
do they open	*potkhim*	פותחים
does he open	*hu poteyakh*	הוא פותח
does it open	*ze niftakh*	זה נפתח
does the store open	*niftakhat hekhanut*	נפתחת החנות
Even so, when can we meet?	*matay bekhol zot nipagesh?*	**מתי בכל זאת ניפגש?**
today	*hayom*	היום
tomorrow	*makhar*	מחר
yesterday	*etmol*	אתמול
last night	**emesh**	אמש
the day before yesterday	*shilshom*	שלשום

in the morning	*baboker*	בבוקר
in the evening	*baerev*	בערב
during the day	*bayom*	ביום
at night	*balayla*	בלילה
early	*mukdam*	מוקדם
at one o'clock	*beshaa akhat*	בשעה אחת
at two, three o'clock	*beshaa shtaim, shalosh*	בשעה שתיים, שלוש
at four o'clock	*beshaa arba*	בשעה ארבע
at five o'clock	*beshaa khamesh*	בשעה חמש
at six o'clock	*beshaa shesh*	בשעה שש
at seven o'clock	*beshaa sheva*	בשעה שבע
at eight o'clock	*beshaa shmone*	בשעה שמונה
at nine o'clock	*beshaa tesha*	בשע תשעה
at ten o'clock	*beshaa eser*	בשעה עשר
at eleven o'clock	*beshaa akhat esre*	בשעה אחת עשרה
at twelve o'clock	*beshaa shteim esre*	בשעה שתים עשרה
at six thirty	*beshaa shesh vakhetsi*	בשעה שש וחצי
at a quarter past six	*beshaa shesh vareva*	בשעה שש ורבע
at a quarter to six	*beshaa reva leshesh*	בשעה רבע לשש
at ten past six	*beshaa shesh veasara*	בשעה שש ועשרה

at twenty to seven	*beshaa esrim lesheva*	בשעה עשרים לשבע
at ten to seven	*beshaa asara lesheva*	בשעה עשרה לשבע
early	*mukdam*	מוקדם
late	*meukhar*	מאוחר
right on time	*bediyuk bazman*	בדיוק בזמן
when	*kaasher*	כאשר
before	*lifney*	לפני
after	*akharey, leakhar*	אחרי, לאחר
in...	*beod...*	**בעוד...**
a day	*yom*	יום
two days	*yomaim*	יומיים
three days	*shlosha yamim*	שלושה ימים
four days	*arbaa yamim*	ארבעה ימים
five days	*khamisha yamim*	חמישה ימים
six days	*shisha yamim*	שישה ימים
a week	*shavua*	שבוע
two weeks	*shvuaim*	שבועיים
three weeks	*shlosha shvuot*	שלושה שבועות
a year	*shana*	שנה
two years	*shnataim*	שנתיים
on (day)...	*beyom...*	ביום...
Sunday	*rishon (alef)*	ראשון (אלף)
Monday	*sheni (bet)*	שני (בית)
Tuesday	*shlishi (gimel)*	שלישי (גימל)
Wednesday	*revii (dalet)*	רביעי (דלת)
Thursday	*khamishi (hey)*	חמישי (הי)

Friday	*shishi (vav)*	שישי (וו)
Saturday	*shabat*	שבת
after...	*akharey*	...אחרי
afterwards	*akhar kakh*	אחר כך
another time	*paam akheret*	פעם אחרת
before...	*lifney*	...לפני
in the morning	*lifney hatsohoraim*	לפני הצהריים
in a while	*beod zman ma*	בעוד זמן מה
never	*af paam*	אף פעם
never	*af paam lo*	אף פעם לא
once	*paam*	פעם
until the evening	*ad haerev*	עד הערב
until	*ad*	עד
I never was...	*af paam lo haiti...*	אף פעם לא הייתי...
I have no time	*eyn li zman*	אין לי זמן

■ How (much, many, old)

Quantity

How long?	*kama zman?*	?כמה זמן
How long do I have to wait?	*kama ani tsarikh lekhakot?*	כמה אני צריך לחכות?
How many?	*kama?*	?כמה
How many people were there?	*kama anashim hayu?*	כמה אנשים היו?
How many times?	*kama peamim?*	?כמה פעמים

How many times do I have to say the same thing!	*kama peamim ani tsarikh lomar oto davar!?*	כמה פעמים אני צריך לומר אותו דבר!
How much?	*kama?*	כמה?
How much did you get?	*kama kibalta?*	כמה קבלת?
How much did you take?	*kama lakakhta?*	כמה לקחת?
How much do they give?	*kama notnim?*	כמה נותנים?
How much do you need?	*kama ata tsarikh?*	כמה אתה צריך?
How much do you want?	*kama ata rotse?*	כמה אתה רוצה?
How much does it cost?	*kama ze ole?*	כמה זה עולה?
How much does it weigh?	*kama ze shokel?*	כמה זה שוקל?
How much is it altogether?	*kama sakh hakol?*	כמה סך הכל?
How much is it?	*kama ze?*	כמה זה?
How much will it be?	*kama ze yih"ye?*	כמה זה יהיה?
How old are you? (m.)	*ben kama ata?*	בן כמה אתה?
How old are you? (f.)	*ben kama at*	בן כמה את?
I am, you (m) are, he is...	*ani, ata, hu ben...*	אני, אתה, הוא בן...
you (f.), she is... years old	*at, hi bat...*	**את, היא בת...**
one	*shana*	שנה

two	*shnataim*	שנתיים
three	*shalosh shanim*	שלוש שנים
four	*arba*	ארבע
five	*khamesh*	חמש
six	*shesh*	שש
seven	*sheva*	שבע
eight	*shmone*	שמונה
nine	*teysha*	תשע
ten	*eser*	עשר
eleven	*akhat esre*	אחת עשרה
twelve	*shteim esre*	שתים עשרה
thirteen	*shlosh esre*	שלוש עשרה
fourteen	*arba esre*	ארבע עשרה
fifteen	*khamesh esre*	חמש עשרה
sixteen	*shesh esre*	שש עשרה
seventeen	*shva esre*	שבע עשרה
eighteen	*shmone esre*	שמונה עשרה
nineteen	*tsha esre*	תשע עשרה
twenty	*esrim*	עשרים
twenty one	*esrim veakhat*	עשרים ואחת
twenty two	*esrim ushtaim*	עשרים ושתיים
twenty three	*esrim veshalosh*	עשרים ושלוש
thirty	*shloshim*	שלושים
thirty one	*shloshim veakhat*	שלושים ואחת
forty	*arbaim*	ארבעים
fifty	*khamishim*	חמישים
sixty	*shishim*	שישים
seventy	*shiv"im*	שבעים

eighty	shmonim	שמונים
ninety	tishim	תשעים
one hundred	mea	מאה
a bit	tipa	טיפה
a bit more	od ktsat	עוד קצת
a certain amount	kamut mesuyemet	כמות מסויימת
a certain number	mispar mesuyam	מספר מסויים
cheap	zol	זול
very cheap	zol meod	זול מאוד
enough	maspik	מספיק
a good few years	kama shanim tovot	כמה שנים טובות
in a while	od meat	עוד מעט
it's expensive	ze yakar	זה יקר
less	pakhot	פחות
less than	pakhot me...	פחות מ...
a little	meat, ktsat	מעט, קצת
a lot	harbe	הרבה
a lot, a large number/ amount	hamon, mispar gadol	המון, מספר גדול
more	od, yoter	עוד, יותר
more than	yoter measher	יותר מאשר
number of	kama	כמה
several times	kama peamim	כמה פעמים
a small number/ amount	mispar katan	מספר קטן
time after time	paam akharey paam	פעם אחרי פעם

too	*miday*	מדי
too little	*meat miday*	מעט מדי
too long	*yoter miday arokh*	יותר מדי ארוך
too much/too many	*yoter miday*	יותר מדי

QUALITY

How?	*eykh?*	איך?
How are things?	*ma nishma?*	מה נשמע?
How are you? (m.)	*ma shlomkha?*	מה שלומך?
How are you? (f.)	*ma shlomekh?*	מה שלומך?
How are you? (m.)	*eykh ata?*	איך אתה?
How did it happen?	*eykh ze kara?*	איך זה קרה?
How do you do?	*eykh holekh?*	איך הולך?
How are you feeling? (f.)	*eykh at margisha?*	איך את מרגישה?
How are you feeling? (m.)	*eykh ata margish?*	איך אתה מרגיש?
How do you get to....?	*eykh magiim el...?*	איך מגיעים אל...?
How do you like this? (m.)	*eykh ze motse khen beeynekha?*	איך זה מוצא חן בעיניך?
How do I know? (m.)	*meeyfo ani yodea?*	מאיפה אני יודע?
How do I know? (f.)	*meeyfo ani yodaat?*	מאיפה אני יודעת?
How do you say?	*eykh omrim?*	איך אומרים?
How does he, she look?	*eykh hu nir"a?, hi nir"et?*	איך הוא נראה?, היא נראת?
How does it look?	*eykh ze nir"a?*	איך זה נראה?
How does one do it?	*eykh osim et ze?*	איך עושים את זה?
How is everything?	*ma hainyanim?*	מה העניינים?

How is it?	eykh ze?	איך זה?
How is it going?	eykh ze holekh?	איך זה הולך?
How must/should I understand this?	eykh lehavin et hadavar haze?	איך להבין את הדבר הזה?
How was it?	eykh ha*ya*?	**איך היה?**
alone	levad	לבד
and so, well	uvkhen	ובכן
as, like...	kfi she..., kmo she...	...כפי ש..., כמו ש
bad	ra	רע
by	al yad*ey*	על-ידי
disgusting	mag"il	מגעיל
everything is fine	hak*ol* beseder	הכל בסדר
excellent	metsuyan	מצויין
for sure	bat*u*akh	בטוח
good	tov	טוב
hesitatingly	im hisusim	עם היסוסים
horrible	nora	נורא
non-stop	lel*o* hefsek	ללא הפסק
not so much	lo kol kakh	לא כל כך
nothing can be done	eyn ma laas*ot*	אין מה לעשות
OK	beseder	בסדר
how do you do it?	eykh ata ose et ze?	**איך אתה עושה את זה?**
often	leitim krov*ot*	לעיתים קרובות
openly	begal*uy*	בגלוי
passive	sav*il*	סביל
perfectly fine	beseder gam*ur*	בסדר גמור
publicly	befumb*ey*	בפומבי

secretly	*bekhashay*	בחשאי
seldom, rarely	*leitim rekhokot*	לעיתים רחוקות
so-so	*kakha kakha*	ככה ככה
sometimes	*lif'amim*	לפעמים
this way	*kakh, kakha*	כך, ככה
till the end	*ad hasof*	עד הסוף
very	*meod*	מאוד
very bad	*ra meod*	רע מאוד
very good, very well	*tov meod*	טוב מאוד
with the help of...	*beezrat...*	בעזרת...
without hesitation	*lelo hisus*	ללא היסוס
wonderful	*nehedar*	נהדר
with God's will	*beezrat hashem*	בעזרת השם
thank God	*barukh hashem*	ברוך השם
I do it this way	*ani ose et ze kakh*	אני עושה את זה ככה
How is he, she?	*eykh hu, hi*	איך הוא, היא?
He looks...	*hu nir"e...*	הוא נראה...
She looks...	*hi nir"it...*	**היא נראת...**
big	*gadol, gdola*	גדול, גדולה
fresh	*raanan, reanana; tari, triya*	רענן, רעננה; טרי, טריה
healthy	*bari, briya*	בריא, בריאה
narrow	*tsar, tsara*	צר, צרה
old (age)	*zaken, zkena*	זקן, זקנה
old	*yashan, yeshana*	ישן, ישנה
poor	*ani, aniya*	עני, עניה
rich	*ashir, ashira*	עשיר, עשירה

short (m.) (f.)	*namukh, nemukha*	נמוך, נמוכה
sick	*khole, khola*	חולה, חולה
small	*katan, ktana*	קטן, קטנה
tall	*gavoa, gvoha*	גבוה, גבוהה
tired	*ayef, ayefa*	עייף, עייפה
wide	*rakhav, rekhava*	רחב, רחבה
young	*tsair, tseira*	צעיר, צעירה
How are you (m.)?	*ma shlomkha?*	?מה שלומך
How are you (f.)?	*ma shlomekh?*	?מה שלומך
I'm fine.	*shlomi tov*	.שלומי טוב

■ WHICH, WHAT (kind of)
COLORS, TASTES

What kind of...?	**eize min...?**	?...איזה מין
like this (m.)	*kaze*	כזה
like this (f.)	*kazot*	כזאת
some kind of (m.)	**eyze shehu**	איזה שהוא
some kind of (f.)	*eyzo shehi*	איזו שהיא
the kind that if...	*kaze sheim...*	...כזה שאם
the kind that when...	*kaze shekaasher...*	...כזה שכאשר
the type that...	*kaze she...*	...כזה ש
the type that you wouldn't want	*kaze shelo tirtse*	כזה שלא תרצה
What flavor?	**eyze taam**	?איזה טעם
What kind of...?	**eyze...?**	**?...איזה**
man is he	*adam hu*	אדם הוא
employer is he	*oved hu*	עובד הוא

What kind?	*eyze min?*	?איזה מין
What sort?	*eyze sug?*	?איזה סוג
What does it taste like?	*eyze taam yesh lo?*	?איזה טעם יש לו
what...	*eyze...*	**...איזה**
depth	*omek*	עומק
height	*gova*	גובה
length	*orekh*	אורך
weight	*mishkal*	משקל
width	*rokhav*	רוחב
which (m.)?	*eyze?*	?איזה
which (f.)?	*eyzo?*	?איזו
which (pl.)?	*eylu?*	?אילו
which color?	*eyze tseva?*	?איזה צבע
colors: (m., f.)	*tsvaim:*	**:צבעים**
black	*shakhor, shkhora*	שחור, שחורה
blue	*kakhol, khula*	כחול, כחולה
brown	*khum, khuma*	חום, חומה
gray	*afor, afora*	אפור, אפורה
green	*yarok, yeruka*	ירוק, ירוקה
orange	*katom, ktuma*	כתום, כתומה
red	*adom, aduma*	אדום, אדומה
white	*lavan, levana*	לבן, לבנה
yellow	*tsahov, tsehuba*	צהוב, צהובה
tastes: (m., f.)	*teamim*	**:טעמים**
fatty	*shamen, shmena*	שמן, שמנה
fresh	*tari, triya*	טרי, טריה
instant	*names, nemesa*	נמס, נמסה
natural	*tiv"i, tiv"it*	טבעי, טבעית

salty (m.)	*maluakh*	מלוח
salty (f.)	*melukha*	מלוחה
sour (m.)	*khamuts*	חמוץ
sour (f.)	*khamutsa*	חמוצה
spicy	*kharif, kharifa*	חריף, חריפה
sweet	*matok, metuka*	מתוק, מתוקה
spoiled (m.)	*mekulkal*	מקולקל
spoiled (f.)	*mekulkelet*	מקולקלת
tasty	*taim, teima*	טעים, טעימה
attributes:	*tkhunot:*	**תכונות:**
arrogant (m.)	*shakhtsan*	שחצן
arrogant (f.)	*shakhtsanit*	שחצנית
bad	*ra, raa*	רע, רעה
brave	*amits, amitsa*	אמיץ, אמיצה
careful	*zahir, zhira*	זהיר, זהירה
careless (m.)	*rashlan,*	רשלן,
careless (f.)	*rashlanit*	רשלנית
disappointed (m.)	*meukhzav,*	מאוכזב,
disappointed (f.)	*meukhzevet*	מאוכזבת
external (m.)	*khitsoni,*	חיצוני,
external (f.)	*khitsonit*	חיצונית
going wild, rowdy	*mitparea (raat)*	מתפרע(ת)
good	*tov, tova*	טוב, טובה
heavy	*kaved, kveda*	כבד, כבדה
intelligent, wise	*khakham,*	חכם,
	khakhama	חכמה
internal	*pnimi, pnimit*	פנימי, פנימית
light	*kal, kala*	קל, קלה

long (m.)	arokh	ארוך
long (f.)	aruka	ארוכה
modest	tsanua, tsnua	צנוע, צנועה
orderly, neat (m.)	mesudar	מסודר
orderly, neat (f.)	mesuderet	מסודרת
quick, alert, active	zariz, zriza	זריז, זריזה
religious	dati, datiya	דתי, דתיה
rough (m.)	mekhuspas	מחוספס
rough (f.)	mekhuspeset	מחוספסת
secular	khiloni, khilonit	חילוני, חילונית
short (f.) (length)	ktsara	קצרה
short (m.)	katsar,	קצר,
short (f.) (height)	nemukha	נמוכה
short (m.)	namukh	נמוך
slow	iti, itit	איטי, איטית
snob (f.)	mitnaset	מתנשאת
snob (m.)	mitnase,	מתנשא,
strong	khazak, khazaka	חזק, חזקה
tall	gavoa, gvoha	גבוה, גבוהה
weak	khalash, khalasha	חלש, חלשה
worthwhile	shave, shava	שווה, שווה

■ Why

Weather, Seasons

Why?	*lama?*	?למה
Why?	*lama, madua?*	?למה, מדוע
Why is that?	*lama ze?*	?למה זה
Why should...I?	*lama...li?*	**?למה...לי**
you (m., f.)	*lekha, lakh*	לך
he	*lo*	לו
she	*la*	לה
We	*lanu*	לנו
you (pl.)	*lakhem*	לכם
they	*lahem*	להם
Why not?	*lama lo?*	?למה לא
Why this way?	*lama kakha*	?למה ככה
Why are you angry (nervous)?	*lama ata mitragez (atsbani)?*	למה אתה מתרגז (עצבני)?
Why are you excited?	*lama ata mitragesh?*	למה אתה מתרגש?
Why are you here?	*lama ata kan?*	?למה אתה כאן
Why are you telling me this?	*lama ata omer li?*	למה אתה אומר לי?
Why aren't you listening?	*lama ata lo makhshiv?*	למה אתה לא מחשיב?
Why don't you have...?	*lama eyn lekha, lakh...?*	?...למה אין לך
Why did this happen?	*lama ze kara?*	?למה זה קרה
Why is it...?	*lama ze...?*	**?...למה זה**
cold	*kar*	קר

dangerous	*mesukan*	מסוכן
dark	*khoshekh*	חושך
hot	*kham*	חם
wet	*ratuv*	רטוב
Why...?	*lama...?*	**למה...?**
aren't we doing anything	*lo osim shum davar*	לא עושים שום דבר
can't you hear anything	*lo shomim shum davar*	לא שומעים שום דבר
do we need	*anakhnu tsrikhim*	אנחנו צריכים
do you say	*ata omer*	אתה אומר
do you want (m.)(f.)	*ata rotse, at rotsa*	אתה רוצה, את רוצה
aren't you answering	*ata lo one*	אתה לא עונה
aren't you saying	*ata lo omer*	אתה לא אומר
isn't there anyone here	*eyn af ekhad*	אין אף אחד?
isn't he here	*hu eynenu*	הוא איננו
can't we get an answer	*i efshar lekabel tshuva*	אי אפשר לקבל תשובה
Why is it forbidden?	*lama asur*	למה אסור?
all because of...	*hakol biglal*	הכל בגלל...
because...	*mipney she..., ki...*	מפני ש..., כי...
because of me	*biglali*	בגללי
because of you (m.)	*biglalkha*	בגללך
because of you (f.)	*biglalekh*	בגללך
because of him	*biglalo*	בגללו
because of her	*biglala*	בגללה

because of us	*biglaleynu*	בגללנו
because of you (pl.)	*biglalkhem*	בגללכם
because of them	*biglalam*	בגללם
this is for...	*ze bishvil...*	**זה בשביל...**
for me	*bishvili*	בשבילי
for you (m.)	*bishvilkha*	בשבילך
for you (f.)	*bishvilekh*	בשבילך
for him	*bishvilo*	בשבילו
for her	*bishvila*	בשבילה
for us	*bishvileynu*	בשבילנו
for you (pl.)	*bishvilkhem*	בשבילכם
for them	*bishvilam*	בשבילם
for, in order to	*kdey*	כדי
I am here because...	*ani kan mipney she...*	אני כאן מפני ש...
I'm excited because...	*ani mitragesh ki...*	אני מתרגש כי...
It angers me that...	*margiz oti she...*	מרגיז אותי ש...
This place is good for me.	*tov li kan*	טוב לי כאן.
so that, in order	*bishvil, bematara, al mnat*	בשביל, במטרה, על מנת
that is because...	*ze biglal she...*	זה בגלל ש...
because I don't have	*biglal she eyn li*	בגלל שאין לי
because...	*ki...*	**כי...**
it is nighttime now	*akhshav layla*	עכשיו לילה
there is no electricity	*eyn khashmal*	אין חשמל
because of...	*biglal...*	**בגלל...**
the dust	*haavak*	האבק
the rain	*hageshem*	הגשם

the sea	*hayam*	הים
(it's) summertime	*hakayits*	הקיץ
the sun	*hashemesh*	השמש
the weather	*mezeg haavir*	מזג האוויר
the wind	*haruakh*	הרוח
the heatwave	*hekhamsin*	החמסין
the winter	*hakhoref*	החורף
because...	*ki...*	**...כי**
everybody is busy	*kulam asukim*	כולם עסוקים
everyone went out	*kulam yatsu*	כולם יצאו
it isn't interesting	*lo meanyen*	לא מעניין
nobody came	*af ekhad lo ba*	אף אחד לא בא
because...	*biglal...*	**...בגלל**
I am afraid (m.)	*sheani pokhed*	שאני פוחד
I am afraid (f.)	*sheani pokhedet*	שאני פוחדת
nobody cares	*shelo ikhpat*	שלא איכפת
	leaf ekhad	לאף אחד
of the noise	*haraash*	הרעש

Verb conjugation in Hebrew is based on additions made to the root of the verb, which is usually consists of three letters.. Hebrew verbs in the present don't change according to pronouns but rather by gender (masculine and feminine) and quantity (singular and plural).In the book the present tense is placed before past and future. In the future and past tenses each person and gender has particular prefixes and suffixes.

The table below shows the structure of verbs in the past, present and future.

Verb in Hebrew	Transliteration	Verb in English
present tense		

	masculine		feminine		
singular		xxxx	singular	...t	תxxxx
plural	...im	םxxxx	plural	...ot	תוxxxx

		past		future	
I	ani	...ti	תיxxx	(e)a...	xxxא
you (m.)	ata	...ta	תxxx	t...	xxxת
you (f.)	at	...t	תxxx	t...i	תxxxי
he	hu	...	xxx	y...	xxxי
she	hi	...a	הxxx	t...	xxxת
we	anakhnu	...nu	נוxxx	n...	xxxנ
you (pl.)	atem	...tem	תםxxx	t...u	תxxxו
they	hem	...u	וxxx	y...u	יxxxו

■ TO AGREE (with...)

להסכים
lehaskim

Present (m.) | Present (f.)

(s)	*maskim*	מסכים	*maskima*	מסכימה
(pl)	*maskimim*	מסכימים	*maskimot*	מסכימות

Past | Future

I	ani	*hiskamti*	הסכמתי	*askim*	אסכים
you (m.)	ata	*hiskamta*	הסכמת	*taskim*	תסכים
you (f.)	at	*hiskamt*	הסכמת	*taskimi*	תסכימי
he	hu	*hiskim*	הסכים	*yaskim*	יסכים
she	hi	*hiskima*	הסכימה	*taskim*	תסכים
we	anakhnu	*hiskamnu*	הסכמנו	*naskim*	נסכים
you (pl.)	atem	*hiskamtem*	הסכמתם	*taskimu*	תסכימו
they	hem	*hiskimu*	הסכימו	*yaskimu*	יסכימו

Agree, do you agree?	*maskim*	מסכים?
I don't agree!	*ani lo maskim*	אני לא מסכים!
Don't agree...	*al taskim*	**אל תסכים...**
with me	*iti*	איתי
with you (m.)	*itkha*	איתך
with you (f.)	*itakh*	איתך
with him	*ito*	איתו
with her	*ita*	איתה
with us	*itanu*	איתנו
with you (pl.)	*itkhem*	איתכם
with you (pl.f.)	*itkhen*	איתכן

with them	*itam*	איתם
with them (f.)	*itan*	איתן
Is (was) agreed...	*muskam*	**מוסכם...**
between us	*beyneynu*	בינינו
between you (pl.)	*beyneykhem*	ביניכם
between them	*beynam*	בינם
agreement	*haskama, heskem*	הסכמה, הסכם

■ TO ANSWER

לענות
laanot

	Present (m.)		Present (f.)	
(s)	*one*	עונה	*ona*	עונה
(pl)	*onim*	עונים	*onot*	עונות

		Past		Future	
I	*ani*	*aniti*	עניתי	*aane*	אענה
you (m.)	*ata*	*anita*	ענית	*taane*	תענה
you (f.)	*at*	*anit*	ענית	*taani*	תעני
he	*hu*	*ana*	ענה	*yaane*	יענה
she	*hi*	*anta*	ענתה	*taane*	תענה
we	*anakhnu*	*aninu*	ענינו	*naane*	נענה
you (pl.)	*atem*	*anitem*	עניתם	*taanu*	תענו
they	*hem*	*anu*	ענו	*yaanu*	יענו

to answer, reply	*laanot*	**לענות**
by chance	*bemikre*	במקרה

correctly	*nakhon*	נכון
implying	*beremez*	ברמז
imprecisely	*lo meduyak*	לא מדויק
impulsively	*bifzizut*	בפזיזות
in other words	*bemilim akherot*	במילים אחרות
incorrectly	*lo nakhon*	לא נכון
indirectly	*beakifin*	בעקיפין
on purpose	*bekhavana*	בכוונה
precisely	*meduyak*	מדויק
quickly	*maher*	מהר
slowly	*leat*	לאט
straight	*yashar*	ישר
the question	*lashaela*	לשאלה
an answer	*tshuva (maane)*	תשובה
a question	*sheela*	שאלה

■ TO APPROACH (people)

לפנות
lifnot

	Present (m.)		Present (f.)	
(s)	*pone*	פונה	*pona*	פונה
(pl)	*ponim*	פונים	*ponot*	פונות

		Past		Future	
I	*ani*	*paniti*	פניתי	*efne*	אפנה
you (m.)	*ata*	*panita*	פנית	*tifne*	תפנה
you (f.)	*at*	*panit*	פנית	*tifni*	תפני

he	hu	pana	פנה	yifne	יפנה
she	hi	panta	פנתה	tifne	תפנה
we	anakhnu	paninu	פנינו	nifne	נפנה
you (pl.)	atem	panitem	פניתם	tifnu	תפנו
they	hem	panu	פנו	yifnu	יפנו

I approached...	paniti	**פניתי...**
the...	el...	אל...
cashier	kupait	קופאית
director, manager	menahel	מנהל
guide	madrikh	מדריך
information (office)	modiin	מודיעין
saleswoman	mokheret	מוכרת
secretary	mazkira	מזכירה
stewardess	dayelet	דיילת
waiter	hameltsar	המלצר
I contacted travel agency.	paniti el sokhnut nesiot	פניתי אל סוכנות נסיעות.
I contacted travel agent.	paniti el sokhenet nesiot	פניתי אל סוכנת נסיעות.
in order to...	bishvil...; bikhdey...	**בשביל...; בכדי...**
ask	lishol	לשאול
find out	levarer	לברר
about...the ticket	al... hakartisim	על...הכרטיסים
the flight	hatisa	הטיסה
the possibilities	haefsharuyot	האפשרויות
the price	hamkhir	המחיר
the trip	hanesiya	הנסיעה

■ TO ASCEND
■ TO COST
■ TO GO UP
■ TO IMMIGRATE TO ISRAEL

לעלות
laalot

	Present (m.)			Present (f.)	
(s)	*ole*	עולה	*ola*		עולה
(pl)	*olim*	עולים	*olot*		עולות

		Past		Future	
I	*ani*	*aliti*	עליתי	*eale*	אעלה
you (m.)	*ata*	*alita*	עלית	*taale*	תעלה
you (f.)	*at*	*alit*	עלית	*taali*	תעלי
he	*hu*	*ala*	עלה	*yaale*	יעלה
she	*hi*	*alta*	עלתה	*taale*	תעלה
we	*anakhnu*	*alinu*	עלינו	*naale*	נעלה
you (pl.)	*atem*	*alitem*	עליתם	*taalu*	תעלו
they	*hem*	*alu*	עלו	*yaalu*	יעלו

it, this, that...	*ze, zot*	**זה, זאת...**
above...	*meal...*	מעל...
from...	*min, meha...*	מן, מה...
by...	*be...*	ב...
on...	*al...*	על...
to...	*el...*	אל...
to...	*le...*	ל...

I (ascended/went up/ immigrated and all others Past Tenses)...	aliti	עליתי...
by elevator	bemaalit	במעלית
to Jerusalem	lirushalaum	לירושלים
by stairs	bamadregot	במדרגות
to the roof	lemaale hagag	למעלה הגג
to lookout	lamitspe	למצפה
up the hill	bamidron	במדרון
by cable car	berakhbal	ברכבל
by path	bashvil	בשביל
How much does it cost?	kama ze ole	כמה זה עולה
the price rose, went up	hamkhir ala	המחיר עלה
I went up the steps to the second floor	aliti bamadregot lakoma hashniya	עליתי במדרגות לקומה השניה
increase, immigration to Israel	aliya	עליה
cost	alut	עלות
cost him a lot	ala lo beyoker	עלה לו ביוקר
(he) was able	ala beyadav	עלה בידיו
(he) wasn't able	lo ala beyadav	לא עלה בידיו
was cheap	ala bezol	עלה בזול

■ TO ASK (questions)
■ TO APPLY FOR

לבקש
levakesh

	Present (m.)		Present (f.)	
(s)	mevakesh	מבקש	mevakeshet	מבקשת
(pl)	mevakshim	מבקשים	mevakshot	מבקשות

		Past		Future	
I	ani	bikashti	בקשתי	avakesh	אבקש
you (m.)	ata	bikashta	בקשת	tevakesh	תבקש
you (f.)	at	bikasht	בקשת	tevakshi	תבקשי
he	hu	bikesh	בקש	yevakesh	יבקש
she	hi	biksha	בקשה	tevakesh	תבקש
we	anakhnu	bikashnu	בקשנו	nevakesh	נבקש
you (pl.)	atem	bikashtem	בקשתם	tevakshu	תבקשו
they	hem	bikshu	בקשו	yevakshu	יבקשו

I am asking for..., I am applying for...	ani mevakesh...	...אני מבקש
an apartment	dira	דירה
a doctor	rofe	רופא
food	**ok**hel	אוכל
help	ezra	עזרה
money	kesef	כסף
I want to arrange a meeting.	ani mevakesh lik**bo**a pgisha	אני מבקש לקבוע פגישה.

hihgly demanded, popular, wanted	*mevukash*	מבוקש
request	*bakasha*	בקשה
please	*bevakasha*	בבקשה
demand	*bikush*	ביקוש

■ TO ASK

לשאול
lish"ol

Present (m.)			Present (f.)		
(s)	*shoel*	שואל	*shoelet*	שואלת
(pl)	*shoalim*	שואלים	*shoalot*	שואלות

		Past		Future	
I	*ani*	*shaalti*	שאלתי	*esh"al*	אשאל
you (m.)	*ata*	*shaalta*	שאלת	*tish"al*	תשאל
you (f.)	*at*	*shaalt*	שאלת	*tish"ali*	תשאלי
he	*hu*	*shaal*	שאל	*yish"al*	ישאל
she	*hi*	*shaala*	שאלה	*tish"al*	תשאל
we	*anakhnu*	*shaalnu*	שאלנו	*nish"al*	נשאל
you (pl.)	*atem*	*shaaltem*	שאלתם	*tish"alu*	תשאלו
they	*hem*	*shaalu*	שאלו	*yish"alu*	ישאלו

Are you asking something?	*ata shoel mashehu?*	אתה שואל משהו?
What are you asking?	*ma ata shoel*	מה אתה שואל?

What are you asking about?	*al ma ata shoel*	?על מה אתה שואל
What is the question?	*ma hasheela?*	?מה השאלה
I want to ask...	*ani rotse lishol...*	אני רוצה לשאול...
how?	*eykh?*	?איך
what?	*ma?*	?מה
when?	*matay?*	?מתי
where?	*eyfo?*	?איפה
which?	*eyze?*	?איזה
who?	*mi?*	?מי
why?	*lama?*	?למה
with whom?	*im mi?*	?עם מי
question	*sheela*	שאלה
request, wish	*mish"ala*	מישאלה
questionnaire	*sheelon*	שאלון
question mark	*siman sheela*	סימן שאלה
your question	*sheelatkha*	שאלתך
in regard to your question	*lesheelatkha*	לשאלתך

■ TO ASK FOR
■ TO DEMAND

לדרוש
lidrosh

Present (m.)		Present (f.)	
(s)	*doresh*	דורש	*doreshet*	דורשת
(pl)	*dorshim*	דורשים	*dorshot*	דורשות

		Past		Future	
I	*ani*	*darashti*	דרשתי	*edrosh*	אדרוש
you (m.)	*ata*	*darashta*	דרשת	*tidrosh*	תדרוש
you (f.)	*at*	*darasht*	דרשת	*tidreshi*	תדרשי
he	*hu*	*darash*	דרש	*yidrosh*	ידרוש
she	*hi*	*darsha*	דרשה	*tidrosh*	תדרוש
we	*anakhnu*	*darashnu*	דרשנו	*nidrosh*	נדרוש
you (pl.)	*atem*	*darashtem*	דרשתם	*tidreshu*	תדרשו
they	*hem*	*darshu*	דרשו	*yidreshu*	ידרשו

to demand...	*lidrosh...*	לדרוש
all the time	*kol hazman*	כל הזמן
immediately	*miyad*	מיד
only	*rak*	רק
the same thing	*oto davar*	אותו דבר
something else	*mashehu akher*	משהו אחר
to be accepted	*lehitkabel*	להתקבל
to get an answer	*latet li tshuva*	לקבל תשובה
request	*drisha*	דרישה
wanted	*darush*	דרוש
popular, in demand	*nidrash*	נדרש
regards	*drishat shalom*	דרישת שלום

■ TO BE, EXIST (mood, weather, time, events)

להיות
*lih"**yot***

		Past		Future	
I	*ani*	*hayiti*	הייתי	*eh"**ye***	אהיה
you (m.)	*ata*	*hayita*	היית	*tih"**ye***	תהיה
you (f.)	*at*	*hayit*	היית	*tih"**yi***	תיהיי
he	*hu*	*haya*	היה	*yih"**ye***	יהיה
she	*hi*	*hayta*	היתה	*tih"**ye***	תהיה
we	*anakhnu*	*hayinu*	היינו	*nih"**ye***	נהיה
you (pl.)	*atem*	*hayitem*	הייתם	*tih"**yu***	תהיו
they	*hem*	*hayu*	היו	*yih"**yu***	יהיו

it was...	**ha*ya*...**	**...היה**
bad	*ra*	רע
cold	*kar*	קר
correct	*nakh**on***	נכון
dangerous	*mesuk**an***	מסוכן
dark	*kh**o**shekh*	חושך
day	*yom*	יום
difficult	*kash**e***	קשה
disgusting	*mag"**il***	מגעיל
early	*mukd**am***	מוקדם
easy	*kal*	קל
in the evening	*erev*	ערב
good	*tov*	טוב
hot	*kham*	חם
incorrect	*lo nakh**on***	לא נכון

late	*meukhar*	מאוחר
in the morning	*boker*	בוקר
nice	*nekhmad*	נחמד
nice	*yafe*	יפה
nighttime	*laila*	לילה
at noon	*tsohoraim*	צהריים
not OK!	*lo beseder*	לא בסדר
OK	*beseder*	בסדר
scary	*mafkhid*	מפחיד
strange	*muzar*	מוזר
windy	*ruakh*	רוח
it was...	*haya...*	**...היה**
light	*or*	אור
he (she), it, there was...	*haya, hayta...*	**...היה, היתה**
arrogant	*shakhtsan, shakhtsanit*	שחצן, שחצנית
attractive	*moshekh, moshekhet*	מושך, מושכת
closed	*sagur, sgura*	סגור, סגורה
coarse, rude	*gas, gas ruakh*	גס, גס רוח
cute	*khamud, khamuda*	חמוד, חמודה
deep	*amok, amuka*	עמוק, עמוקה
disgusting	*mag"il, mag"ila*	מגעיל, מגעילה
enough	*maspik*	מספיק
not enough	*lo maspik*	לא מספיק
exciting	*meragesh*	מרגש
feels	*margish, margisha*	מרגיש, מרגישה
all for nothing	*lashav*	לשווא

future	*atid*	עתיד
generous	*nadiv, nediva*	נדיב, נדיבה
happy	*meushar,*	מאושר,
	meusheret	מאושרת
happy	*sameyakh, smekha*	שמח, שמחה
(a) holiday	*khag*	חג
in the past	*beavar*	בעבר
likable	*khaviv, khaviva*	חביב, חביבה
lost	*avud, avuda*	אבוד, אבודה
modest	*tsanua, tsnua*	צנוע, צנועה
naughty	*shovav, shoveva*	שובב, שובבה
had nerve	*khutspan,*	חוצפן,
	khutspanit	חוצפנית
nice, good looking	*yafe, yafa*	יפה, יפה
cut in the open	*galuy, gluya*	גלוי, גלויה
polite	*adiv, adiva*	אדיב, אדיבה
practical	*maasi, maasit*	מעשי, מעשית
sad	*atsuv, atsuva*	עצוב, עצובה
sensitive	*ragish, regisha*	רגיש, רגישה
serious	*retsini, retsinit*	רציני, רצינית
serious, grave	*khamur, khamura*	חמור, חמורה
shallow	*radud, reduda*	רדוד, רדודה
smooth	*khalak, khalaka*	חלק, חלקה
strange	*muzar, muzara*	מוזר, מוזרה
stingy	*kamtsan, kamtsanit*	קמצן, קמצנית
stubborn	*akshan, akshanit*	עקשן, עקשנית
too much	*yoter miday*	יותר מדי
misserable	*umlal, umlala*	אומלל, אומללה

unnecessary	*meyutar*	מיותר
very...	*meod...*	מאד...
interesting	*meanyen*	מעניין
there was a/an...	*hayta...*	**היתה ...**
embitterment	*hitmarmerut*	התמרמרות
exam	*bkhina*	בחינה
excitement	*hitragshut*	התרגשות
happiness	*simkha*	שמחה
hatred	*sin"a*	שנאה
meeting (important)	*pgisha khashuva*	פגישה חשובה
mistake	*taut*	טעות
problem	*baaya*	בעיה
Sabbath	*shabat*	שבת
serious illness	*makhala kasha*	מחלה קשה
strange reaction	*tguva muzara*	תגובה מוזרה
war	*milkhama*	מלחמה
being that...	*heyot ve...*	היות ו...
It was felt.	*haya murgash*	היה מורגש.
It was in the past.	*haya beavar*	היה בעבר.
There will be in the future.	*yih"ye beatid*	יהיה בעתיד.
it depended on...	*haya taluy be*	היה תלוי ב...
What was it (that)?	*ma ze haya?*	מה זה היה?
it was to do with...	*haya kashur le...*	היה קשור ל...

■ TO BE ABLE TO

יכול
yakhol

	Present (m.)			Present (f.)	
(s)	*yakhol*	יכול		*yekhola*	יכולה
(pl)	*yekholim*	יכולים		*yekholot*	יכולות

		Past		Future	
I	*ani*	*yakholti*	יכולתי	*ukhal*	אוכל
you (m.)	*ata*	*yakholta*	יכולת	*tukhal*	תוכל
you (f.)	*at*	*yakholt*	יכולת	*tukhli*	תוכלי
he	*hu*	*yakhol*	יכול	*yukhal*	יוכל
she	*hi*	*yakhla*	יכלה	*tukhal*	תוכל
we	*anakhnu*	*yakholnu*	יכולנו	*nukhal*	נוכל
you (pl.)	*atem*	*yakholtem*	יכולתם	*tukhlu*	תוכלו
they	*hem*	*yakhlu*	יכלו	*yukhlu*	יוכלו

can...	*yakhol...*	**יכול...**
answer	*laanot*	לענות
ask	*lish"ol*	לשאול
do	*laasot*	לעשות
go	*lalekhet*	ללכת
pay	*leshalem*	לשלם
understand	*lehavin*	להבין
can(not) be	*(lo)yakhol lihyot*	(לא) יכול להיות
capability	*yakholet*	יכולת
He has ability.	*yesh lo yekholet*	יש לו יכולת.

■ TO BE AFRAID (from..., of...)

לפחד
lefakhed

Present (m.)

(s)	*mefakhed*	מפחד
(pl)	*mefakhdim*	מפחדים

Present (f.)

mefakhedet	מפחדת
mefakhdot	מפחדות

Past / Future

		Past		Future	
I	ani	*pakhadti*	פחדתי	*afakhed*	אפחד
you (m.)	ata	*pakhadta*	פחדת	*tefakhed*	תפחד
you (f.)	at	*pakhadt*	פחדת	*tefakhdi*	תפחדי
he	hu	*pakhad*	פחד	*yifakhed*	יפחד
she	hi	*pakhada*	פחדה	*tefakhed*	תפחד
we	anakhnu	*pakhadnu*	פחדנו	*nefakhed*	נפחד
you (pl.)	atem	*pakhadtem*	פחדתם	*tefakhdu*	תפחדו
they	hem	*pakhadu*	פחדו	*yifakhdu*	יפחדו

from...	*mi, min...*	...מ, מן
that...	*she...*	ש...
the situation	*hamatsav*	המצב
I'm afraid...	*ani mefakhed...*	אני מפחד...
to drive	*linhog*	לנהוג
to fly	*latus*	לטוס
to swim in the sea	*liskhot bayam*	לשחות בים
that she...	*shehi...*	**שהיא...**
won't come	*lo tavo*	לא תבוא
won't understand	*lo tavin*	לא תבין
doesn't want	*lo tirtse*	לא תרצה

don't be afraid	*al tefakh**ed***	אל תפחד
fear	*pakhad*	פחד

■ TO BE HAPPY
■ TO BE GLAD

לשמוח
*lism**o**akh*

Present (m.)			Present (f.)	
(s)	*sam**ey**akh*	שמח	*smekha*	שמחה
(pl)	*smekhim*	שמחים	*smekhot*	שמחות

		Past		Future	
I	*ani*	*samakhti*	שמחתי	*esmakh*	אשמח
you (m.)	*ata*	*samakhta*	שמחת	*tismakh*	תשמח
you (f.)	*at*	*samakht*	שמחת	*tismekhi*	תשמחי
he	*hu*	*samakh*	שמח	*yismakh*	ישמח
she	*hi*	*samkha*	שמחה	*tismakh*	תשמח
we	*anakhnu*	*samakhnu*	שמחנו	*nismakh*	נשמח
you (pl.)	*atem*	*samakhtem*	שמחתם	*tismekhu*	תשמחו
they	*hem*	*samkhu*	שמחו	*yismekhu*	ישמחו

I'm happy..., I'm glad...	*ani sam**ey**akh...*	**...אני שמח**
to meet you	*lehakir otkha*	להכיר אותך
to be here	*lihy**o**t kan*	להיות כאן
to visit Israel	*levak**er** beisrael*	לבקר בישראל
in Jerusalem	*birushalaim*	בירושלים
to be happy...	*lism**o**akh...*	לשמוח...

a lot of the time	*harbe zman*	הרבה זמן
in vain	*lashav*	לשוא
together	*beyakhad*	ביחד
with all (his, her...) heart	*bekhol halev*	בכל הלב
good news	*yedia mesamakhat*	ידיעה משמחת
happiness	*simkha*	שמחה
gladly	*besimkha*	בשמחה

■ TO BE IN PAIN

לכאוב
likh"ov

Present (m.)			Present (f.)	
(s)	*koev*	כואב	*koevet*	כואבת
(pl)	*koavim*	כואבים	*koavot*	כואבות

	Past			Future	
I	*ani*	*kaavti*	כאבתי		
you (m.)	*ata*	*kaavta*	כאבת		
you (f.)	*at*	*kaavt*	כאבת		
he	*hu*	*kaav*	כאב	*yikh"av*	יכאב
she	*hi*	*kaava*	כאבה	*tikh"av*	תכאב
we	*anakhnu*	*kaavnu*	כאבנו		
you (pl.)	*atem*	*kaavtem*	כאבתם		
they	*hem*	*kaavu*	כאבו	*yikh"avu*	יכאבו

pain	*keev*	כאב
Does it hurt here?	*koev kan?*	?כואב כאן

| I am in pain | koev li? | כואב לי |
| Are you in pain? | koev lekha? | ?כואב לך |

■ TO BE LATE (for...)

לאחר
leakher

Present (m.)		Present (f.)	
(s) *meakher*	מאחר	*meakheret*	מאחרת
(pl) *meakhrim*	מאחרים	*meakhrot*	מאחרות

		Past		Future	
I	*ani*	*ikharti*	אחרתי	*eakher*	אאחר
you (m.)	*ata*	*ikharta*	אחרת	*teakher*	תאחר
you (f.)	*at*	*ikhart*	אחרת	*teakhri*	תאחרי
he	*hu*	*ikher*	אחר	*yeakher*	יאחר
she	*hi*	*ikhra*	אחרה	*teakher*	תאחר
we	*anakhnu*	*ikharnu*	אחרנו	*neakher*	נאחר
you (pl.)	*atem*	*ikhartem*	אחרתם	*teakhru*	תאחרו
they	*hem*	*ikhru*	אחרו	*yeakhru*	יאחרו

to be late...	*leakher...*	**...לאחר**
for the bus	*laotobus*	לאוטובוס
for the meeting	*lapgisha*	לפגישה
for the plane	*lamatos*	למטוס
for the train	*larakevet*	לרכבת
for work	*leavoda*	לעבודה

to be a few minutes late	*bekhama dakot*	בכמה דקות
The plane is running late.	*hamatos meakher*	.המטוס מאחר

■ TO BRING

להביא
lehavi

Present (m.)			Present (f.)		
(s)	*mevi*	מביא	*mevia*	מביאה
(pl)	*meviim*	מביאים	*meviot*	מביאות

		Past		Future	
I	*ani*	*heveti*	הבאתי	*avi*	אביא
you (m.)	*ata*	*heveta*	הבאת	*tavi*	תביא
you (f.)	*at*	*hevet*	הבאת	*tavii*	תביאי
he	*hu*	*hevi*	הביא	*yavi*	יביא
she	*hi*	*hevia*	הביאה	*tavi*	תביא
we	*anakhnu*	*hevenu*	הבאנו	*navi*	נביא
you (pl.)	*atem*	*hevetem*	הבאתם	*taviu*	תביאו
they	*hem*	*heviu*	הביאו	*yaviu*	יביאו

Please bring me a gift/present.	*tavi li bevakasha matana*	תביא לי בבקשה מתנה.
Don't bring anything.	*al tavi klum*	אל תביא כלום.
brought	*muva*	מובא
imported	*meyuva*	מיובא

introduction	*mavo*	מבוא
prophet	*navi*	נביא

■ TO BUY (cosmetics, clothes, products) לקנות
liknot

Present (m.)			Present (f.)	
(s)	*kone*	קונה	*kona*	קונה
(pl)	*konim*	קונים	*konot*	קונות

		Past		Future	
I	*ani*	*kaniti*	קניתי	*ekne*	אקנה
you (m.)	*ata*	*kanita*	קנית	*tikne*	תקנה
you (f.)	*at*	*kanit*	קנית	*tikni*	תקני
he	*hu*	*kana*	קנה	*yikne*	יקנה
she	*hi*	*kanta*	קנתה	*tikne*	תקנה
we	*anakhnu*	*kaninu*	קנינו	*nikne*	נקנה
you (pl.)	*atem*	*kanitem*	קניתם	*tiknu*	תקנו
they	*hem*	*kanu*	קנו	*yiknu*	יקנו

What are you buying?	*ma ata kone*	?מה אתה קונה
Where did you buy this?	*eyfo kanita et ze*	?איפה קנית את זה
I want to buy...	*ani rotse liknot...*	**...אני רוצה לקנות**
body lotion	*krem guf*	קרם גוף
cosmetics	*tamrukim*	תמרוקים
lipstick	*odem*	אודם
perfume	*bosem*	בושם

shampoo	*shampo*	שמפו
soap	*sabon*	סבון
suntan lotion	*krem shizuf*	קרם שיזוף
food:	*okhel*	אוכל:
bread	*lekhem*	לחם
fruit	*perot*	פרות
meat	*basar*	בשר
dairy products	*motsrey khalav*	מוצרי חלב
vegetables	*yerakot*	ירקות
a bag	*tik*	תיק
everything thats necessary	*kol ma shedarush*	כל מה שדרוש
record	*taklit*	תקליט
book, books	*sefer, sfarim*	ספר, ספרים
something to eat	*mashehu leekhol*	משהו לאכול
tablecloth	*mapat shulkhan*	מפת שולחן
I want to buy...	*ani rotse liknot...*	**אני רוצה לקנות...**
clothing:	*bgadim:*	בגדים:
boots	*magafaim*	מגפיים
a coat	*meil*	מעיל
a hat	*kova*	כובע
jeans	*jins*	ג'ינס
pants	*mikhnasayim*	מכנסיים
a shirt	*khultsa*	חולצה
shoes	*naalaim*	נעליים
a skirt	*khatsait*	חצאית
socks	*garbaim*	גרביים
a sweater	*sveder*	סוודר

a singlet	*gufiya*	גופייה
underwear	*levanim*	לבנים
a bathing suit	*beged yam*	בגד ים
a clock	*shaon*	שעון
a comb	*masrek*	מסרק
a pin	*sika*	סיכה
purchase	*kniya*	קניה
a ticket	*kartis*	כרטיס
an umbrella	*mitriya*	מטרייה

■ TO CALL
■ TO GET IN TOUCH

להתקשר
lehitkasher

	Present (m.)		Present (f.)	
(s)	*mitkasher*	מתקשר	*mitkasheret*	מתקשרת
(pl)	*mitkashrim*	מתקשרים	*mitkashro*	מתקשרות

		Past		Future	
I	*ani*	*hitkasharti*	התקשרתי	*etkasher*	אתקשר
you (m.)	*ata*	*hitkasharta*	התקשרת	*titkasher*	תתקשר
you (f.)	*at*	*hitkashart*	התקשרת	*titkashri*	תתקשרי
he	*hu*	*hitkasher*	התקשר	*yitkasher*	יתקשר
she	*hi*	*hitkashra*	התקשרה	*titkasher*	תתקשר
we	*anakhnu*	*hitkasharnu*	התקשרנו	*nitkasher*	נתקשר
you (pl.)	*atem*	*hitkashartem*	התקשרתם	*titkashru*	תתקשרו
they	*hem*	*hitkashru*	התקשרו	*yitkashru*	יתקשרו

by phone	*betelephon*	בטלפון
next week	*beshavua haba*	שבוע הבא
today	*hayom*	היום
tomorrow	*makhar*	מחר
urgent	*dakhuf*	דחוף
yesterday	*etmol*	אתמול
we'll be in touch	*nih"ye bekesher*	נהיה בקשר
for	*bishvil*	בשביל
in order to	*kdey*	כדי
with	*im*	עם
connection, line, touch	*kesher*	קשר
the connection was cut off	*hakesher nutak*	הקשר נותק
call me	*titkasher elay*	תתקשר אלי

■ TO CHOOSE

לבחור
livkhor

Present (m.)			Present (f.)	
(s)	*bokher*	בוחר	*bokheret*	בוחרת
(pl)	*bokhrim*	בוחרים	*bokhrot*	בוחרות

		Past		Future	
I	*ani*	*bakharti*	בחרתי	*evkhar*	אבחר
you (m.)	*ata*	*bakharta*	בחרת	*tivkhar*	תבחר
you (f.)	*at*	*bakhart*	בחרת	*tivkheri*	תבחרי
he	*hu*	*bakhar*	בחר	*yivkhar*	יבחר
she	*hi*	*bakhra*	בחרה	*tivkhar*	תבחר
we	*anakhnu*	*bakharnu*	בחרנו	*nivkhar*	נבחר
you (pl.)	*atem*	*bakhartem*	בחרתם	*tivkheru*	תבחרו
they	*hem*	*bakhru*	בחרו	*yivkheru*	יבחרו

Choose! (f.)...	*tivkheri...*	**תבחרי...**
the dress	*et hasimla*	את השמלה
the hotel	*et hamalon*	את המלון
the present	*et hamatana*	את המתנה
the room	*et hakheder*	את החדר
the excursion	*et hatiyul*	את הטיול
something	*mashehu*	משהו
for (as) a souviner	*lemazkeret*	למזכרת
whatever you (f.) want	*ma sheat rotsa*	מה שאת רוצה

■ TO CLOSE

לסגור
lisgor

		Present (m.)		Present (f.)	
(s)		*soger*	סוגר	*sogeret*	סוגרת
(pl)		*sogrim*	סוגרים	*sogrot*	סוגרות

		Past		Futue	
I	*ani*	*sagarti*	סגרתי	*esgor*	אסגור
you (m.)	*ata*	*sagarta*	סגרת	*tisgor*	תסגור
you (f.)	*at*	*sagart*	סגרת	*tisgeri*	תסגרי
he	*hu*	*sagar*	סגר	*yisgor*	יסגור
she	*hi*	*sagra*	סגרה	*tisgor*	תסגור
we	*anakhnu*	*sagarnu*	סגרנו	*nisgor*	נסגור
you (pl.)	*atem*	*sagartem*	סגרתם	*tisgeru*	תסגרו
they	*hem*	*sagru*	סגרו	*yisgeru*	יסגרו

closed	*sagur*	סגור
closing	*sgira*	סגירה
frame	*misgeret*	מסגרת
Have we closed the matter?	*sagarnu et hainyan*	סגרנו את העניין?
the matter is closed	*hainyan sagur*	העניין סגור
parentheses, brackets	*sograim*	סוגריים
please close (m.)	*tisgor bevakasha*	תסגור בבקשה
please close (f.)	*tisgeri bevakasha*	תסגרי בבקשה

■ TO COME (places, activities) לבוא
lavo

Present (m.)		Present (f.)	
(s) *ba*	בא	*baa*	באה
(pl) *baim*	באים	*baot*	באות

		Past		Future	
I	*ani*	*bati*	באתי	*avo*	אבוא
you (m.)	*ata*	*bata*	באת	*tavo*	תבוא
you (f.)	*at*	*bat*	באת	*tavoi*	תבואי
he	*hu*	*ba*	בא	*yavo*	יבוא
she	*hi*	*baa*	באה	*tavo*	תבוא
we	*anakhnu*	*banu*	באנו	*navo*	נבוא
you (pl.)	*atem*	*batem*	באתם	*tavou*	תבואו
they	*hem*	*bau*	באו	*yavou*	יבואו

where...from?	*mieyfo*	מאיפה
home	*habayta*	הביתה
to...	*le...*	...ל
from...	*mi, me...*	...מ
from the...	*meha...*	**מה...**
army	*tsava*	צבא
bank	*bank*	בנק
dentist	*rofe shinaim*	רופא שיניים
exhibition, fair	*tetsuga, yerid*	תצוגה, יריד
field, lot	*migrash*	מגרש
a friend	*khaver*	חבר

cinema	*seret*	סרט
office	*misrad*	משרד
partner	*shutaf*	שותף
shop	*khanut*	חנות
station	*takhana*	תחנה
street	*rkhov*	רחוב
this place	*hamakom haze*	המקום הזה
university	*universita*	אוניברסיטה
for half an hour	*lekhatsi shaa*	לחצי שעה
I came...	*ani ba...*	**אני בא...**
to...	*el...*	אל...
to me	*elay*	אלי
to you	*elekha*	אליך
to you (f.)	*elayikh*	אליך
to him	*elav*	אליו
to her	*eleyha*	אליה
to us	*eleynu*	אלינו
to you (pl.)	*eleykhem*	אליכם
to them	*eleyhem*	אליהם
to all this	*el kol ze*	אל כל זה
come to...	*bou el...*	בואו אל...
came...	*ba...*	**בא...**
to clarify	*levarer*	לברר
to do	*laasot*	לעשות
to hear	*lishmoa*	לשמוע
to return (something)	*lehakhzir*	להחזיר
to see	*lir"ot*	לראות
to send	*lishloakh*	לשלוח

to tell	*lesaper*	לספר
to visit	*levaker*	לבקר
to work	*laavod*	לעבוד
for	*bishvil*	בשביל
after	*akharey*	אחרי
again	*od paam*	עוד פעם
alone	*levad*	לבד
already	*kvar*	כבר
another time	*paam akheret*	פעם אחרת
before	*lifney*	לפני
early	*mukdam*	מוקדם
late	*meukhar*	מאוחר
the day after tomorrow	*mokhrotaim*	מחרתיים
the day before yesterday	*shilshom*	שלשום
today	*hayom*	היום
together with...	*yakhad im...*	...יחד עם
tomorrow	*makhar*	מחר
yesterday	*etmol*	אתמול

■ TO CONSULT

להתייעץ

lehit"yaets

	Present (m.)		Present (f.)	
(s)	*mit"yaets*	מתייעץ	*mit"yaetset*	מתייעצת
(pl)	*mit"yatsim*	מתייעצים	*mit"yatsot*	מתייעצות

		Past		Future	
I	*ani*	*hit"yaatsti*	התייעצתי	*et"yaets*	אתייעץ
you (m.)	*ata*	*hit"yaatsta*	התייעצת	*tit"yaets*	תתייעץ
you (f.)	*at*	*hit"yaatst*	התייעצת	*tit"yaetsi*	תתייעצי
he	*hu*	*hit"yaets*	התייעץ	*yit"yaets*	יתייעץ
she	*hi*	*hit"yaatsa*	התייעצה	*tit"yaets*	תתייעץ
we	*anakhnu*	*hit"yaatsnu*	התייעצנו	*nit"yaets*	נתייעץ
you (pl.)	*atem*	*hit"yaatstem*	התייעצתם	*tit"yaatsu*	תתייעצו
they	*hem*	*hit"yaatsu*	התייעצו	*yit"yaatsu*	יתייעצו

about...	*al..., odot...*	...על...., אודות
about something important	*beinyan khashuv*	בעניין חשוב
before making a decision	*lifney hakhlata*	לפני החלטה
If it is worthwhile to...	*haim keday...*	**...האם כדאי**
buy	*liknot*	לקנות
go	*lalekhet*	ללכת
travel	*linsoa*	לנסוע
with...	*im, be...*	...עם, ב
with my wife	*im ishti*	עם אישתי
with my husband	*bebaali*	בבעלי

■ TO COST

לעלות
laalot

	Present (m.)			Present (f.)	
(s)	*ole*	עולה	*ola*	עולה	
(pl)	*olim*	עולים	*olot*	עולות	

		Past		Future	
I	*ani*	*aliti*	עליתי	*aale*	אעלה
you (m.)	*ata*	*alita*	עלית	*taale*	תעלה
you (f.)	*at*	*alit*	עלית	*taali*	תעלי
he	*hu*	*ala*	עלה	*yaale*	יעלה
she	*hi*	*alta*	עלתה	*taale*	תעלה
we	*anakhnu*	*alinu*	עלינו	*naale*	נעלה
you (pl.)	*atem*	*alitem*	תעלו	*taalu*	תעלו
they	*hem*	*alu*	עלו	*yaalu*	יעלו

How much does it cost?	*kama ze ole?*	?כמה זה עולה
It is...	*ze...*	**...זה**
cheap	*bezol*	בזול
expensive	*beyoker*	ביוקר
It costs...	*ze ole...*	**....זה עולה**
10 shekels	*asara shkalim*	עשרה שקלים
$5	*khamisha dolar*	חמשה דולר
the price...	*hamkhir...*	**...המחיר**
rose	*ala*	עלה
will rise	*yaale*	יעלה
may rise	*asuy laalot*	עשוי לעלות

■ TO CROSS
■ TO PASS (places to cross)

לעבור
laavor

Present (m.)			Present (f.)	
(s)	*over*	עובר	*overet*	עוברת
(pl)	*ovrim*	עוברים	*ovrot*	עוברות

		Past		Future	
I	*ani*	*avarti*	עברתי	*eavor*	אעבור
you (m.)	*ata*	*avarta*	עברת	*taavor*	תעבור
you (f.)	*at*	*avart*	עברת	*taavri*	תעברי
he	*hu*	*avar*	עבר	*yaavor*	יעבור
she	*hi*	*avra*	עברה	*taavor*	תעבור
we	*anakhnu*	*avarnu*	עברנו	*naavor*	נעבור
you (pl.)	*atem*	*avartem*	עברתם	*taavru*	תעברו
they	*hem*	*avru*	עברו	*yaavru*	יעברו

to cross...	*laavor et...*	...לעבור את
the bridge	*hagesher*	הגשר
the river	*hanahar*	הנהר
the street	*harkhov*	הרחוב
most of the route	*rov hamaslul*	רוב המסלול
to pass from one topic to another	*laavor minose lenose*	לעבור מנושא לנושא
travel across all the country	*laavor et kol haarets*	לעבור את כל הארץ
from Galilee to the Dead Sea	*mihagalil ad yam hamelakh*	מהגליל עד ים המלך

from the Mediterranean	*mihayam hatikhon*	מהים התיכון
Sea to the Jordan River	*ad nahar yarden*	עד נהר ירדן
safely	*beshalom*	בשלום

■ TO CUT

לחתוך
lakhtokh

Present (m.)

(s)	*khotekh*	חותך
(pl)	*khotkhim*	חותכים

Present (f.)

khotekhet	חותכת
khotkhot	חותכות

Past / Future

		Past		Future	
I	*ani*	*khatakhti*	חתכתי	*akhtokh*	אחתוך
you (m.)	*ata*	*khatakhta*	חתכת	*takhtokh*	תחתוך
you (f.)	*at*	*khatakht*	חתכת	*takhtekhi*	תחתכי
he	*hu*	*khatakh*	חתך	*yakhtokh*	יחתוך
she	*hi*	*khatkha*	חתכה	*takhtokh*	תחתוך
we	*anakhnu*	*khatakhnu*	חתכנו	*nakhtokh*	נחתוך
you (pl.)	*atem*	*khatakhtem*	חתכתם	*takhtekhu*	תחתכו
they	*hem*	*khatkhu*	חתכו	*yakhtekhu*	יחתכו

Please cut me...	*takhtokh li bevakasha...*	תחתוך לי בבקשה...
here	*kan*	כאן
kilo	*kilo*	קילו
half a kilogram of meat	*khatsi kilo basar*	חצי קילו בשר
a kilo and a half	*kilo vakhetsi*	קילו וחצי

two kilos	*shney kilo*	שני קילו
two and a half	*shnaim vakhetsi*	שניים וחצי
three kilos	*shalosh kilo*	שלוש קילו
...piece	*khatikha*	**חתיכה...**
far	*shmena*	שמנה
heavy	*kveda*	כבדה
light	*kala*	קלה
narrow	*tsara*	צרה
thick (m., f.)	*ave, ava*	עבה, עבה
thin (m., f.)	*dak, daka*	דק, דקה
wide (f.)	*rekhava*	רחבה
salami	*naknik*	נקניק
a slice of bread	*prusat lekhem*	פרוסת לחם
some cheese	*gvina tsehuba*	גבינה צהובה
this rope	*et hakhevel haze*	את החבל הזה
watermelon	*avatiyakh*	אבטיח
until the end	*ad hasof*	עד הסוף
little by little	*ktsat ktsat*	קצת קצת
bit by bit	*tipin tipin*	טיפין טיפין
everything	*hakol*	הכל
quick(ly)	*maher*	מהר
very slowly	*leat leat*	לאט לאט
straight	*yashar*	ישר
from the side	*betsad*	בצד
smooth	*khalak*	חלק
a cut	*khatakh*	חתך
is cut	*khatukh*	חתוך
piece	*khatikha*	חתיכה

cutting	*khitukh*	חיתוך
with a ...khife	*besakin...*	בסכין...
sharp	*khada*	חדה
blunt	*lo mekhudedet*	לא מחודדת

■ TO DECIDE

להחליט
lehakhlit

	Present (m.)		**Present (f.)**	
(s)	*makhlit*	מחליט	*makhlita*	מחליטה
(pl)	*makhlitim*	מחליטים	*makhlitot*	מחליטות

		Past		**Future**	
I	*ani*	*hekhlatti*	החלטתי	*akhlit*	אחליט
you (m.)	*ata*	*hekhlatta*	החלטת	*takhlit*	תחליט
you (f.)	*at*	*hekhlatt*	החלטת	*takhliti*	תחליטי
he	*hu*	*hekhlit*	החליט	*yakhlit*	יחליט
she	*hi*	*hekhlita*	החליטה	*takhlit*	תחליט
we	*anakhnu*	*hekhlatnu*	החלטנו	*nakhlit*	נחליט
you (pl.)	*atem*	*hekhlattem*	החלטתם	*takhlitu*	תחליטו
they	*hem*	*hekhlitu*	החליטו	*yakhlitu*	יחליטו

We decided...	*hekhlatnu*	**החלטנו...**
to stay	*lehishaer*	להישאר
to go out	*latset*	לצאת
We'll make a decision (decide)...	*nakhlit...*	**נחליט...**
about it	*al kakh*	על כך

soon	*od meat*	עוד מעט
after...	*akharey...*	אחרי...
we see...	*shenir"e*	**שנראה...**
all the information	*et kol hanetunim*	את כל הנתונים
all the papers (documents)	*hamismakhim*	המסמכים

■ TO DESCEND
■ TO GO DOWN

לרדת
laredet

Present (m.)			Present (f.)	
(s)	*yored*	יורד	*yoredet*	יורדת
(pl)	*yordim*	יורדים	*yordot*	יורדות

		Past		Future	
I	*ani*	*yaradti*	ירדתי	*ered*	ארד
you (m.)	*ata*	*yaradta*	ירדת	*tered*	תרד
you (f.)	*at*	*yaradt*	ירדת	*terdi*	תרדי
he	*hu*	*yarad*	ירד	*yered*	ירד
she	*hi*	*yarda*	ירדה	*tered*	תרד
we	*anakhnu*	*yaradnu*	ירדנו	*nered*	נרד
you (pl.)	*atem*	*yaradtem*	ירדתם	*terdu*	תרדו
they	*hem*	*yardu*	ירדו	*yerdu*	ירדו

down	*lemata*	למטה
from you (m.)	*mimkha*	ממך

from you (f.)	*mimekh*	ממך
gradually	*behadraga*	בהדרגה
into	*letokh*	לתוך
safely	*batuakh*	בטוח
slowly	*leat*	לאט
to	*el*	אל
descend, decline, emigration from Israel	*yerida*	ירידה
go down immediately	*red miyad*	רד מיד
get off of me!	*red mimeni!*	!רד ממני
the prices dropped	*hamkhirim yardu*	המחירים ירדו

■ TO DO

לעשות
laasot

Present (m.)		Present (f.)	
(s) *ose*	עושה	*osa*	עושה
(pl) *osim*	עושים	*osot*	עושות

		Past		Future	
I	*ani*	*asiti*	עשיתי	*eese*	אעשה
you (m.)	*ata*	*asita*	עשית	*taase*	תעשה
you (f.)	*at*	*asit*	עשית	*taasi*	תעשי
he	*hu*	*asa*	עשה	*yaase*	יעשה
she	*hi*	*asta*	עשתה	*taase*	תעשה
we	*anakhnu*	*asinu*	עשינו	*naase*	נעשה

you (pl.)	*atem*	*asitem*	עשיתם	*taasu*	תעשו
they	*hem*	*asu*	עשו	*yaasu*	יעשו

do as you wish	*ase kirtsonkha*	עשה כרצונך
do me a favour...	*ase li tova...*	...עשה לי טובה
close the window	*sgor et hekhalon*	סגור את החלון
open the door	*tiftakh et hadelet*	תפתח את הדלת
everything	*hakol*	הכל
a little, a bit	*meat*	מעט
many, much	*harbe*	הרבה
not to do anything	*lo laasot shum davar*	לא לעשות שום דבר
nothing	*shum davar*	שום דבר
What are you doing?	*ma ata ose*	?מה אתה עושה
What can I do?	*ma laasot*	מה לעשות
What have you done?	*me asita*	!מה עשית
What is there to do?	*ma tsarikh laasot*	?מה צריך לעשות
What will we do about it?	*ma naase banadon*	מה נעשה בנדון
deed, act	*maase*	מעשה
doing, acting, activity	*asiya*	עשיה
done	*asuy*	עשו

■ TO DRINK   (beverages)

לשתות
lishtot

		Present (m.)		Present (f.)	
(s)		*shote*	שותה	*shota*	שותה
(pl)		*shotim*	שותים	*shotot*	שותות

		Past		Future	
I	*ani*	*shatiti*	שתיתי	*eshte*	אשתה
you (m.)	*ata*	*shatita*	שתית	*tishte*	תשתה
you (f.)	*at*	*shatit*	שתית	*tishti*	תשתי
he	*hu*	*shata*	שתה	*yishte*	ישתה
she	*hi*	*shateta*	שתתה	*tishte*	תשתה
we	*anakhnu*	*shatinu*	שתינו	*nishte*	נשתה
you (pl.)	*atem*	*shatitem*	שתיתם	*tishtu*	תשתו
they	*hem*	*shatu*	שתו	*yishtu*	ישתו

I am thirsty.	*ani tsame*	אני צמא.
I want to drink.	*ani rotse lishtot*	אני רוצה לשתות.
I'll drink something.	*eshte mashehu*	אשתה משהו.
In summer you drink a lot.	*bekayitz shotim harbe*	בקיץ שותים הרבה.
Let me drink...	*ten li lishtot...*	**תן לי לשתות...**
beer	*bira*	בירה
beverage	*shtiya*	שתייה
brandy	*brandi*	ברנדי
coffee	*kafe*	קפה
cognac	*kon"yak*	קוניאק

Cola, Tempo, Kinley	*kola, tempo, kinli*	קולה, טמפו, קינלי
malt beer	*bira shkhora*	בירה שחורה
milk	*khalav*	חלב
raspberry juice	*petel*	פטל
tea	*te*	תה
vodka	*vodka*	וודקה
water	*maim*	מים
cold water	*maim karim*	מים קרים
wine	*yain*	יין
pour me...	*timzog li...*	**תמזוג לי...**
...juice	*mitz...*	**מיץ...**
apple	*tapukhey etz*	תפוחי עץ
grape	*anavim*	ענבים
grapefruit	*eshkoliyot*	אשכוליות
lemon	*limon*	לימון
orange	*tapuzim*	תפוזים
tomato	*agvaniyot*	עגבניות

■ TO EAT (food: fruits, vegetables...)

לאכול
leekhol

	Present (m.)		Present (f.)	
(s)	okhel	אוכל	okhelet	אוכלת
(pl)	okhlim	אוכלים	okhlot	אוכלות

		Past		Future	
I	ani	akhalti	אכלתי	okhal	אוכל
you (m.)	ata	akhalta	אכלת	tokhal	תאכל
you (f.)	at	akhalt	אכלת	tokhli	תאכלי
he	hu	akhal	אכל	yokhal	יאכל
she	hi	akhla	אכלה	tokhal	תאכל
we	anakhnu	akhalnu	אכלנו	nokhal	נאכל
you (pl.)	atem	akhaltem	אכלתם	tokhlu	תאכלו
they	hem	akhlu	אכלו	yokhlu	יאכלו

breakfast	arukhat boker	ארוחת בוקר
dinner	arukhat erev	ארוחת ערב
lunch	arukhat tsohorayim	ארוחת צהריים
portion	mana	מנה
second portion	mana shniya	מנה שניה
side-dish, addition	tosefet	תוספת
barley	grisim	גריסים
biscuit, cookies	biskvit, ugiyot	בסקוויט, עגיות
bread	lekhem	לחם
butter	khem"a	חמאה
cake	uga	עוגה

chicken	*of*	עוף
coffee	*kafe*	קפה
instant coffee	*nes kafe*	נס קפה
dairy (kashrut)	*khalavi*	חלבי
drink	*shtiya*	שתייה
egg	*beytsa*	ביצה
fried egg	*khavita*	חביתה
felafel	*falafel*	פלאפל
fish	*dagim*	דגים
pickled fish	*dag maluakh*	דג מלוח
frankfurter	*naknikiya*	נקניקיה
frankfurters	*naknikiyot*	נקניקיות
French fries	*tchips*	ציפס
fruit	*perot*	פרות
ice cream	*glida*	גלידה
jam	*riba*	ריבה
leben	*leben*	לבן
meat	*basar*	בשר
meat (kashrut)	*basari*	בשרי
milk	*khalav*	חלב
oil	*shemen*	שמן
patties	*ktsitsot*	קציצות
potatoes	*tapukhey adama*	תפוחי אדמה
rice	*orez*	אורז
roast	*tsli*	צלי
roasted meat in pita	*shvarma*	שוורמה
salad	*salat*	סלט
salami	*naknik*	נקניק

salt	*melakh*	מלח
soup	*marak*	מרק
sour cream	*shamenet*	שמנת
steak	*stek, umtza*	סטיק, אומצה
sugar	*sukar*	סוכר
tea	*te*	תה
turkey	*hodu*	הודו
vegetables	*yerakot*	ירקות
vinegar	*khometz*	חומץ
cream cheese	*gvina levana*	גבינה לבנה
cheese	*gvina tsehuba*	גבינה צהובה
yogurt	*eshel, leben*	אשל, לבן
fruit:	*perot*	**פרות:**
apple	*tapuakh*	תפוח
apples	*tapukhey etz*	תפוחי עץ
banana	*banana*	בננה
bananas	*bananot*	בננות
grapefruit	*eshkolit*	אשכולית
grapefruits	*eshkoliyot*	אשכוליות
grapes	*anavim*	ענבים
melon	*melon*	מלון
orange	*tapuz*	תפוז
oranges	*tapuzim*	תפוזים
peach	*afarsek*	אפרסק
peaches	*afarsekim*	אפרסקים
pear	*agas*	אגס
pears	*agasim*	אגסים
plum	*shezif*	שזיף

plums	shezifim	שזיפים
tangerine oranges	klemantinot	קלמנטינות
watermelon	avatiyakh	אבטיח
vegetables:	yerakot	ירקות:
beet	selek	סלק
cabbage	kruv	כרוב
carrot	gezer	גזר
corn	tiras	תירס
cucumber	melafefon	מלפפון
cucumbers	melafefonim	מלפפונים
eggplant	khatsilim	חצילים
olives	zeytim	זיתים
onion	batsal	בצל
pepper	pilpel	פלפל
tomato	agvaniya	עגבניה
tomatoes	agvaniyot	עגבניות
zuccini	kishuim	קישואים
nuts	egozim	אגוזים
sunflower seeds	garinim	גרעינים
...juice	mits	מיץ...
apple	tapukhim	תפוחים
grape	anavim	ענבים
lemon	limon	לימון
orange	tapuzim	תפוזים
raspberry	petel	פטל
food	okhel	אוכל
eating	akhila	אכילה

■ TO ENTER (places to enter)

להיכנס
lehikanes

		Present (m.)		Present (f.)	
(s)		*nikhnas*	נכנס	*nikhneset*	נכנסת
(pl)		*nikhnasim*	נכנסים	*nikhnasot*	נכנסות

		Past		Future	
I	*ani*	*nikhnasti*	נכנסתי	*ekanes*	אכנס
you (m.)	*ata*	*nikhnasta*	נכנסת	*tikanes*	תיכנס
you (f.)	*at*	*nikhnast*	נכנסת	*tikansi*	תיכנסי
he	*hu*	*nikhnas*	נכנס	*yikanes*	יכנס
she	*hi*	*nikhnesa*	נכנסה	*tikanes*	תיכנס
we	*anakhnu*	*nikhnasnu*	נכנסנו	*nikanes*	ניכנס
you (pl.)	*atem*	*nikhnastem*	נכנסתם	*tikansu*	תיכנסו
they	*hem*	*nikhnesu*	נכנסו	*yikansu*	יכנסו

among, between	*beyn*	בין
to me	*elay*	אלי
to you	*elekha*	אליך
to him	*elav*	אליו
to her	*eleha*	אליה
to us	*eleynu*	אלינו
to you (pl.)	*eleykhem*	אליכם
to them	*eleyhem*	אליהם
please come in	*tikanes bevakasha*	תיכנס בבקשה
entered...	*nikhnas...*	**נכנס...**
alone	*levad*	לבד

his room	*elav lakheder*	אליו לחדר
inside	*pnima*	פנימה
to the doctor's office	*larofe*	לרופא
to the office	*lamisrad*	למשרד
to passport control	*labikoret darkonim*	לביקורת דרכונים
to the bar	*labar*	לבאר
to the bathroom	*lahadar ambatiya*	לחדר אמבטיה
to the bus	*laotobus*	לאוטובוס
to the coffee shop	*lakafe*	לקפה
to the entrance hall	*laolam hanisa*	לאולם הכניסה
to the hotel	*lamalon*	למלון
to the laundry	*lamakhbesa*	למכבסה
to the post office	*ladoar*	לדואר
to the restaurant	*lamis"ada*	למסעדה
to the shelter	*lamiklakhat*	למקלחת
to the toilets	*leshirutim*	לשרותים
to the travel agency	*lesokhnut nesiyot*	לסוכנות נסיעות
to the waiting room	*laolam hamtana*	לאולם המתנה
together with...	*yakhad im...*	יחד עם...

■ TO FALL (from..., on...)　　　　　ליפול
lipol

Present (m.)		Present (f.)	
(s) *nofel*	נופל	*nofelet*	נופלת
(pl) *noflim*	נופלים	*noflot*	נופלות

		Past		Future	
I	*ani*	*nafalti*	נפלתי	*epol*	אפול
you (m.)	*ata*	*nafalta*	נפלת	*tipol*	תיפול
you (f.)	*at*	*nafalt*	נפלת	*tipli*	תיפלי
he	*hu*	*nafal*	נפל	*yipol*	יפול
she	*hi*	*nafla*	נפלה	*tipol*	תיפול
we	*anakhnu*	*nafalnu*	נפלנו	*nipol*	ניפול
you (pl.)	*atem*	*nafaltem*	נפלתם	*tiplu*	תיפלו
they	*hem*	*naflu*	נפלו	*yiplu*	יפלו

on the floor	*al haritspa*	על הריצפה
from above	*milemala*	מלמעלה
from the chair	*mehakise*	מהכיסא
from the stairs	*mehamadregot*	מהמדרגות
from the table	*mehashulkhan*	מהשולחן
a fall (in the)	*nefila beshaar*	נפילה בשער
exchange rate	*hakhalifin*	החליפין

■ TO FEEL (feelings, pains)

להרגיש
lehargish

Present (m.)			Present (f.)	
(s)	*margish*	מרגיש	*margisha*	מרגישה
(pl)	*margishim*	מרגישים	*margishot*	מרגישות

		Past		Future	
I	*ani*	*hirgashti*	הרגשתי	*argish*	ארגיש
you (m.)	*ata*	*hirgashta*	הרגשת	*targish*	תרגיש
you (f.)	*at*	*hirgasht*	הרגשת	*targishi*	תרגישי
he	*hu*	*hirgish*	הרגיש	*yargish*	ירגיש
she	*hi*	*hirgisha*	הרגישה	*targish*	תרגיש
we	*anakhnu*	*hirgashnu*	הרגשנו	*nargish*	נרגיש
you (pl.)	*atem*	*hirgashtem*	הרגשתם	*targishu*	תרגישו
they	*hem*	*hirgishu*	הרגישו	*yargishu*	ירגישו

We feel...	*anakhnu margishim......*	**אנחנו מרגישים......**
very well, fine	*metsuyan*	מצוין
wonderful	*nehedar*	נהדר
I felt that...	*hirgashti...*	**...הרגשתי**
I have a high temperature	*khom*	חום
that I am...	*sheani...*	**...שאני**
slight (m.) weak	*khalash*	חלש
slight (f.) weak	*khalasha*	חלשה
strong (m.)	*khazak*	חזק
strong (f.)	*khazaka*	חזקה

fainting (m.)	*mitalef*	מתעלף
fainting (f.)	*mitalefet*	מתעלפת
getting into trouble (m.)	*mistabekh*	מסתבך
getting into trouble (f.)	*mistabekhet*	מסתבכת
unpleasant	*lo naim*	לא נעים
pain...	*keev...*	**כאב...**
in the chest	*bekhaze*	בחזה
in my left hand	*beyad smalit*	ביד שמאלית
in my left side	*betsad smol*	בצד שמאל
in my leg	*baregel*	ברגל
in my right hand	*beyad yaminit*	ביד ימינית
on my right side	*betsad yamini*	בצד ימין
in my shoulder	*bakatef*	בכתף
nausea	*bekhila*	בחילה
I have headaches.	*yesh li keevey rosh*	יש לי כאבי ראש.
lousy feeling (sl.)	*hargasha mezupetet*	הרגשה מזופטת
wonderful feeling	*hargasha metsuyenet*	הרגשה מצוינת
How do you feel? (sl.)	*eykh hamargash?*	איך המרגש?

■ TO FIND (papers, documents, things)   למצוא
limtso

	Present (m.)			Present (f.)	
(s)	*motse*	מוצא	*motset*		מוצאת
(pl)	*motsim*	מוצאים	*motsot*		מוצאות

		Past		Future	
I	*ani*	*matsati*	מצאתי	*emtsa*	אמצא
you (m.)	*ata*	*matsata*	מצאת	*timtsa*	תמצא
you (f.)	*at*	*matsat*	מצאת	*timtsei*	תמצאי
he	*hu*	*matsa*	מצא	*yimtsa*	ימצא
she	*hi*	*matsa*	מצאה	*timtsa*	תמצא
we	*anakhnu*	*matsanu*	מצאנו	*nimtsa*	נמצא
you (pl.)	*atem*	*matsatem*	מצאתם	*timtseu*	תמצאו
they	*hem*	*matsu*	מצאו	*yimtseu*	ימצאו

bus	**otobus**	אוטובוס
documents/papers:	*mismakhim:*	**מסמכים:**
passport	*darkon*	דרכון
photocopy	*tatslum*	תצלום
driving license	*rishyon nehiga*	רשיון נהיגה
vehicle license	*rishyon rechev*	רשיון רכב
e-mail	**imeyl**	אי מאיל
letter	*mikhtav*	מכתב
taxi	*monit*	מונית
telephone	*telephon*	טלפון
the entrance	*et haknisa*	את הכניסה

the exit	*et hayetsiya*	את היציאה
facsimile, fax	*faks*	פקס
the group	*et hakvutsa*	את הקבוצה
the guide	*et hamadrikh*	את המדריך
the luggage	*et hamit"an*	את המטען
the suitcases	*et hamizvadot*	את המזוודות
the way	*et haderekh*	את הדרך
visa	*viza*	ויזה
bargain	*metsia*	מציאה
He found himself.	*hu matsa et atsmo*	הוא מצא את עצמו.
I can't find anything.	*ani lo motse klum*	אני לא מוצא כלום.
I like it.	*ze motse khen beeynay*	זה מוצא חן בעיניי.
is found, present (m., f.)	*nimtsa, nimtsea*	נמצא, נמצאה
What did you see in her?	*ma matsata ba*	מה מצאת בה?

■ TO FORGET

לשכוח
lishkoakh

	Present (m.)		Present (f.)	
(s)	*shokheakh*	שוכח	*shokhakhat*	שוכחת
(pl)	*shokhakhim*	שוכחים	*shokhakhot*	שוכחות

		Past		Future	
I	*ani*	*shakhakhti*	שכחתי	*eshkakh*	אשכח
you (m.)	*ata*	*shakhakhta*	שכחת	*tishkakh*	תשכח

you (f.)	*at*	*shakhakht*	שכחת	*tishkekhi*	תשכחי
he	*hu*	*shakhakh*	שכח	*yishkakh*	ישכח
she	*hi*	*shakhekha*	שכחה	*tishkakh*	תשכח
we	*anakhnu*	*shakhakhnu*	שכחנו	*nishkakh*	נשכח
you (pl.)	*atem*	*shakhakhtem*	שכחתם	*tishkekhu*	תשכחו
they	*hem*	*shakhekhu*	שכחו	*yishkekhu*	ישכחו

don't forget	*al tishkakh*	אל תשכח
I almost forgot.	*kim"at shakhakhti*	כמעט שכחתי.
I forgot everything.	*shakhakhti et hakol*	שכחתי את הכל.
I never forget.	*af paam*	אף פעם
	lo shakhaakhti	לא שכחתי.
Let's forget what happened.	*nishkakh ma shehaya*	נשכח מה שהיה.
I forgot...	*shakhakhti...*	**...שכחתי**
about this meeting	*al hapgisha hazot*	על הפגישה הזאת
the address	*et haktovet*	את הכתובת
about this thing	*et hadavar haze*	את הדבר הזה
to do	*laasot*	לעשות
to give	*latet*	לתת
to take	*lakakhat*	לקחת
to write	*likhtov*	לכתוב
I completely forgot.	*shakhakhti legamrey*	שכחתי לגמרי.
common, frequent	*shakhiyakh*	שכיח

■ TO FORGIVE

לסלוח
lisloakh

		Present (m.)		Present (f.)	
(s)		*soleyakh*	סולח	*solakhat*	סולחת
(pl)		*solkhim*	סולחים	*solkhot*	סולחות

		Past		Future	
I	*ani*	*salakhti*	סלחתי	*eslakh*	אסלח
you (m.)	*ata*	*salakhta*	סלחת	*tislakh*	תסלח
you (f.)	*at*	*salakht*	סלחת	*tislekhi*	תסלחי
he	*hu*	*salakh*	סלח	*yislakh*	יסלח
she	*hi*	*salkha*	סלחה	*tislakh*	תסלח
we	*anakhnu*	*salakhnu*	סלחנו	*nislakh*	נסלח
you (pl.)	*atem*	*salakhtem*	סלחתם	*tislekhu*	תסלחו
they	*hem*	*salkhu*	סלחו	*yislekhu*	יסלחו

excuse me	*tislakh li bevakasha*	תסלח לי בבקשה
where is...	**ey**fo ze...	...איפה זה
where is the...	**ey**fo nimtsa...	**...איפה נמצא**
hotel	*malon*	מלון
Sorry!	*slakh li*	!סלח לי

■ TO GIVE (small things)

לתת
latet

Present (m.)

(s)	*noten*	נותן
(pl)	*notnim*	נותנים

Present (f.)

notenet	נותנת
notnot	נותות

Past

I	*ani*	*natati*	נתתי
you (m.)	*ata*	*natata*	נתת
you (f.)	*at*	*natat*	נתת
he	*hu*	*natan*	נתן
she	*hi*	*natna*	נתנה
we	*anakhnu*	*natanu*	נתנו
you (pl.)	*atem*	*natatem*	נתתם
they	*hem*	*natnu*	נתנו

Future

eten	אתן
titen	תתן
titni	תתני
yiten	יתן
titen	תתן
niten	ניתן
titnu	תתנו
yitnu	יתנו

give...	*ten...*	תן...
me	*li*	לי
you	*lekha*	לך
you (f.)	*lakh*	לך
him	*lo*	לו
her	*la*	לה
us	*lanu*	לנו
you (pl.)	*lakhem*	לכם
them	*lahem*	להם
give us...	***ten lanu...***	**תן לנו...**
an answer	*tshuva*	תשובה

a card	kartis	כרטיס
a hand	yad	יד
a notebook	makhberet	מחברת
a pen	et	עט
change (money)	odef	עודף
a checkbook	pinkas tchekim	פנקס שקים
resume	korot khaim	קורות חיים
an identity card	teudat zehut	תעודת זהות
an immigration certificate	teudat ole	תעודת עולה
medicine	trufa	תרופה
money	kesef	כסף
passport	darkon	דרכון
the document	et hateuda	את התעודה
this book	et hasefer haze	את הספר הזה
this	et ze	את זה
let me...	*ten li...*	**...תן לי**
answer	laanot	לענות
do	laasot	לעשות
hear	lishmoa	לשמוע
open	liftoakh	לפתוח
understand	lehavin	להבין

■ TO GO (directions, places, activities)

ללכת
lalekhet

Present (m.)			Present (f.)	
(s)	*holekh*	הולך	*holekhet*	הולכת
(pl)	*holkhim*	הולכים	*holkhot*	חולכות

		Past		Future	
I	*ani*	*halakhti*	הלכתי	*elekh*	אלך
you (m.)	*ata*	*halakhta*	הלכת	*telekh*	תלך
you (f.)	*at*	*halakht*	הלכת	*telkhi*	תלכי
he	*hu*	*halakh*	הלך	*yelekh*	ילך
she	*hi*	*halkha*	הלכה	*telekh*	תלך
we	*anakhnu*	*halakhnu*	הלכנו	*nelekh*	נלך
you (pl.)	*atem*	*halakhtem*	הלכתם	*telkhu*	תלכו
they	*hem*	*halkhu*	הלכו	*yelkhu*	ילכו

far	*rakhok*	רחוק
near	*karov*	קרוב
left	*smola*	שמאלה
right	*yamina*	ימינה
where?	*lean*	?לאן
to...	*el...*	...אל
from...	*mi, me, meha...*	...מ, מה
to the/a...	*le...*	**...ל**
bank	*bank*	בנק
barbershop, salon	*maspera*	מספרה
bedroom	*khadar shena*	חדר שינה

bus stop	takhanat **o**tobus	תחנת אוטובוס
center	merk**az**	מרכז
clerk	pak**id**	פקיד
dentist	rof**e** shinaim	רופא שיניים
kitchen	mitb**a**kh	מטבח
park	gan	גן
pool	brekh**a**	בריכה
post office	d**o**ar	דואר
principal, manager	menahel	מנהל
representative	el natsig	אל נציג
restaurant	mis"ad**a**	מסעדה
room	kheder	חדר
seashore, beach	khof hayam, hof	חוף הים, חוף
teacher	more	מורה
I am going around.	ani holekh	אני הולך
	mesav**iv**	מסביב.
to buy...	liknot...	**לקנות...**
juice, water	mits, maim	מיץ, מים
something to eat	mashehu leekh**o**l	משהו לאכול
to check	livd**o**k	לבדוק
to do	laasot	לעשות
to drink	lishtot	לשתות
to eat	leekh**o**l	לאכול
to hear...	lishmoa	**לשמוע...**
a joke	bdikh**a**	בדיחה
the news	khadash**o**t	חדשות
listen to the radio	lishm**o**a radio	לשמוע רדיו
to read	likr**o**	לקרוא

I am going...	*ani holekh*	**...אני הולך**
to take notebook	*lakakhat*	לקחת
	makhberet	מחברת
to rest	*lanuakh*	לנוח
to sleep	*lishon*	לישון
to receive	*lekabel*	לקבל
to return, to refund	*lehakhzir*	להחזיר
to take a shower/bath	*lehitrakhets*	להתרחץ
	bemiklakhat	במקלחת
money	*kesef*	כסף
to clean...	*lenakot*	**...לנקות**
a little	*ktsat*	קצת
the room	*et hakheder*	את החדר
this thing	*et hadavar haze*	את הדבר הזה
these things	*et hadvarim*	את הדברים
	haeylu	האלו
this	*et ze*	את זה

◼ TO HAVE (NEED) TO

להיות צריך
lihyot tsarikh
להצטרך
lehitstarekh

	Present (m.)		Present (f.)	
(s)	*tsarikh*	צריך	*tsrikha*	צריכה
(pl)	*tsrikhim*	צריכים	*tsrikhot*	צריכות

	Past			Future	
I	*hayiti tsarikh*	הייתי צריך	*etstarekh*	אצטרך
you (m.)	*hayita tsarikh*	היית צריך	*titstarekh*	תצטרך
you (f.)	*hayit tsrikha*	היית צריכה	*titstarkhi*	תצטרכי
he	*haya tsarikh*	היה צריך	*yitstarekh*	יצטרך
she	*hayta tsrikha*	הייתה צריכה	*titstarekh*	תצטרך
we	*hayinu tsrikhim*	היינו צריכים	*nitstarekh*	נצטרך
you (pl.)	*hayitem tsrikhim*	הייתם צריכים	*titstarkhu*	תצטרכו
they	*hayu tsrikhim*	היו צריכים	*yitstarkhu*	יצטרכו

I need	*ani tsarikh*	אני צריך
need urgently	*tsarikh dakhuf*	צריך דחוף
need	*tsarikh*	צריך
needs (has) to be	*tsarikh lihyot*	צריך להיות
needs (has) to do	*tsarikh laasot*	צריך לעשות
it is necessary	*tsorekh*	צורך
Who needs it?	*mi tsarikh et ze*	מי צריך את זה?
consumption, demand	*tsrikha*	צריכה
necessity	*mitsrakh*	מצרך

■ TO HEAR

לשמוע
lishmoa

Present (m.)			Present (f.)	
(s)	shomea	שומע	shomaat	שומעת
(pl)	shomim	שומעים	shomot	שומעות

		Past		Future	
I	ani	shamati	שמעתי	eshma	אשמע
you (m.)	ata	shamata	שמעת	tishma	תשמע
you (f.)	at	shamat	שמעת	tishmei	תשמעי
he	hu	shama	שמע	yishma	ישמע
she	hi	sham"a	שמעה	tishma	תשמע
we	anakhnu	shamanu	שמענו	nishma	נשמע
you (pl.)	atem	shamatem	שמעתם	tishmeu	תשמעו
they	hem	sham"u	שמעו	yishmeu	ישמעו

It sounds good.	nishma tov	נשמע טוב.
Do you hear?	shomea	שומע?
Can you hear me?	ata shomea oti?	אתה שומע אותי?
What can you hear?	ma ata shomea	מה אתה שומע?
you hear (f)	at shomaat	את שומעת
rumor(s)	shmua	שמועה
	(shmuot)	(שמועות)
Hear, O Israel!	shma yisrael!	שמע ישראל!
hearing	shmia	שמיעה
How are things?	ma nishma?	מה נשמע?

■ TO HELP (assistance)

לעזור
laazor

	Present (m.)		Present (f.)	
(s)	*ozer*	עוזר	*ozeret*	עוזרת
(pl)	*ozrim*	עוזרים	*ozrot*	עוזרות

		Past		Future	
I	*ani*	*azarti*	עזרתי	*eazor*	אעזור
you (m.)	*ata*	*azarta*	עזרת	*taazor*	תעזור
you (f.)	*at*	*azart*	עזרת	*taazri*	תעזרי
he	*hu*	*azar*	עזר	*yaazor*	יעזור
she	*hi*	*azra*	עזרה	*taazor*	תעזור
we	*anakhnu*	*azarnu*	עזרנו	*naazor*	נעזור
you (pl.)	*atem*	*azartem*	עזרתם	*taazru*	תעזרו
they	*hem*	*azru*	עזרו	*yaazru*	יעזרו

Help me, please... *taazor li bevakasha* **...תעזור לי בבקשה**

to take the suitcases	*lakakhat mizvadot*	לקחת מזוודות
to fill in the form	*lemale et hatofes*	למלא את הטופס
to take out money from the automatic bank teller	*limshokh kesef mikaspomat*	למשוך כסף מכספומט
to read in Hebrew	*likro beivrit*	לקרוא בעברית
to find the place	*limtso et hamakom*	למצוא את המקום
help	*ezra*	עזרה

helping	*ezer*	עזר
maid	*ozeret*	עוזרת
assistant	*ozer*	עוזר

■ TO HOPE

לקוות
lekavot

	Present (m.)		Present (f.)	
(s)	*mekave*	מקווה	*mekava*	מקווה
(pl)	*mekavim*	מקווים	*mekavot*	מקוות

		Past		Future	
I	*ani*	*kiviti*	קיוויתי	*akave*	אקווה
you (m.)	*ata*	*kivita*	קיווית	*tekave*	תקווה
you (f.)	*at*	*kivit*	קיווית	*tekavi*	תקווי
he	*hu*	*kiva*	קיווה	*yekave*	יקווה
she	*hi*	*kivta*	קיוותה	*tekave*	תקווה
we	*anakhnu*	*kivinu*	קיווינו	*nekave*	נקווה
you (pl.)	*atem*	*kivitem*	קיוויתם	*tekavu*	תקווו
they	*hem*	*kivu*	קיוו	*yekavu*	יקווו

let's hope...	*nekave...*	נקווה...
we'll (have time)...	*shenaspik...*	שנספיק...
we'll manage	*shenatsliakh...*	שנצליח...
to see...	*lir"ot...*	לראות...
the performance	*et hahatsaga...*	את ההצגה...
we'll return...	*shenakhzor...*	שנחזור...
on time	*bamoed*	במועד

today	*od hayom*	עוד היום
he'll come on time	*sheyavo bazman*	שיבוא בזמן
it will be OK	*sheyih"ye tov*	שיהיה טוב
that...	*sheod*	**שעוד...**
there's still room	*nish"ar makom*	.נשאר מקום
there are tickets	*sheyesh kartisim*	שיש כרטיסים
we'll have time	*shenaspik*	שנספיק
we'll succeed manage	*shenatsliyakh*	שנצליח

■ TO INVITE (people)
■ TO ORDER (foods)
■ TO BOOK (rooms)

להזמין
lehazmin

Present (m.)		Present (f.)	
(s) *mazmin*	מזמין	*mazmina*	מזמינה
(pl) *mazminim*	מזמינים	*mazminot*	מזמינות

		Past		Future	
I	*ani*	*hizmanti*	הזמנתי	*azmin*	אזמין
you (m.)	*ata*	*hizmanta*	הזמנת	*tazmin*	תזמין
you (f.)	*at*	*hizmant*	הזמנת	*tazmini*	תזמיני
he	*hu*	*hizmin*	הזמין	*yazmin*	יזמין
she	*hi*	*hizmina*	הזמינה	*tazmin*	תזמין
we	*anakhnu*	*hizmanu*	הזמנו	*nazmin*	נזמין
you (pl.)	*atem*	*hizmantem*	הזמנתם	*tazminu*	תזמינו
they	*hem*	*hizminu*	הזמינו	*yazminu*	יזמינו

May I take your order?	*ma tazminu*	?מה תזמינו
What are you ordering?	*ma atem mazminim?*	**מה אתם מזמינים?**
a room for 2 persons	kheder leshnaim	חדר לשניים
a room...	kheder...	...חדר
for 1 night	lelayla ekhad	ללילה אחד
for 2 night	leshtey leylot	לשתי לילות
seasonal salad	salat hauna	סלט העונה
stuffed cabbage	kruv memule	כרוב ממולא
sandwiches with	sendvich im	**סנדוויץ עם**
tuna	tuna	טונה
cheese	gvina	גבינה
salted cheese	gvina mlukha	גבינה מלוחה
cheese	gvina tshuba	גבינה צהובה
omlet	khavita	חביטה
coffee	kafe	קפה
tea	te	תה
with cake	im uga	עם עוגה
juice	mits	מיץ
soup	marak	מרק
main course	mana shniya	מנה שניה
I am inviting you (f.)...	ani mazmin otakh...	**אני מזמין אותך...**
to visit me	elay	אלי
to a show	lehatsaga	להצגה
on a trip	letiyul	לטיול
to see a movie	leseret	לסרט
for a cup of coffee	lekos kafe	לכוס קפה
for a meal	learukha	לארוחה

order	*hazmana*	הזמנה
invited	*muzman*	מוזמן
invited (pl.)	*muzmanim*	מוזמנים
a special invitation	*hazmana*	הזמנה
	meyukhedet	מיוחדת

■ TO LEARN (professions) — ללמוד
lilmod

Present (m.)		Present (f.)	
(s) *lomed*	לומד	*lomedet*	לומדת
(pl) *lomdim*	לומדים	*lomdot*	לומדות

		Past		Future	
I	*ani*	*lamadti*	למדתי	*elmad*	אלמד
you (m.)	*ata*	*lamadta*	למדת	*tilmad*	תלמד
you (f.)	*at*	*lamadt*	למדת	*tilmedi*	תלמדי
he	*hu*	*lamad*	למד	*yilmad*	ילמד
she	*hi*	*lamda*	למדה	*tilmad*	תלמד
we	*anakhnu*	*lamadnu*	למדנו	*nilmad*	נלמד
you (pl.)	*atem*	*lamadtem*	למדתם	*tilmedu*	תלמדו
they	*hem*	*lamdu*	למדו	*yilmedu*	ילמדו

I studied five years to become...	*lamadti khamesh shanim lihyot...*	**למדתי חמש שנים להיות...**
an accountant	*roe kheshbon*	רואה חשבון

to become	*lihyot*	**להיות**
...engineer	*mehandes...*	**...מהנדס**
an automative	*otomatsiya*	אוטומציה
a civil	*ezrakhi*	אזרחי
a communication	*tikshoret*	תקשורת
a computer	*makhshevim*	מחשבים
a construction	*binyan*	בנין
an electrical	*khashmal*	חשמל
an electronics	*elektronika*	אלקטרוניקה
a food	*mazon*	מזון
heating	*hasaka*	הסקה
materials	*khomarim*	חומרים
mechanical	*mekhonot*	מכונות
sewage	*biyuv*	ביוב
train	*rakevet*	רכבת
transport	*takhbura*	תחבורה
chief engineer	*mehandes roshi*	מהנדס ראשי
carpenter	*nagar*	נגר
construction worker	*poel binyan*	פועל בנין
conducter	*mevaker*	מבקר
doctor	*rofe*	רופא
driver	*nahag*	נהג
electrician	*khashmalai*	חשמלאי
mechanic	*mekhonai*	מכונאי
locksmith	*masger*	מסגר
nurse	*akhot*	אחות
production manager	*menahel yetsur*	מנהל ייצור

I studied medicine, specializing in...	*lamadti refua bemegama...*	**למדתי רפואה במגמה...**
children's diseases	*makhalot yeladim*	מחלות ילדים
heart diseases	*makhalot lev*	מחלות לב
infectious diseases	*makhalot medabkot*	מחלות מדבקות
internal	*makhalot pnim*	מחלות פנים
respiratory diseases	*makhalot darkei neshima*	מחלות דרכי נשימה
skin disorders	*makhalot or*	מחלות עור
surgery	*kirurgiya*	כירורגיה
to teach	*lelamed*	ללמד
I taught	*limadti*	לימדתי
teaches (m.) (f.)	*melamed, melamedet*	מלמד, מלמדת
I'll teach...	*elamed...*	אלמד...
a/an... teacher	*more le...*	**מורה ל...**
arithmetic	*kheshbon*	חשבון
Bible	*tanakh*	תנ"ך
biology	*biologia*	ביולוגיה
chemistry	*khimiya*	כימיה
civics	*ezrakhut*	אזרחות
computers	*makhshevim*	מחשבים
exercise, gym	*hit"amlut*	התעמלות
geography	*geografiya*	גיאוגרפיה
history	*historiya*	הסטוריה
language	*lashon*	לשון
Hebrew language	*hasafa haivrit*	השפה העברית
literature	*sifrut*	ספרות

mathematics	*matematika*	מתמטיקה
physics	*fisika*	פיזיקה
classroom	*kitat limud*	כיתת לימוד
it was taught	*nilmad*	נלמד
lecturer	*martse*	מרצה
scholarly	*melumad*	מלומד
text school books	*sifrey limud*	ספרי לימוד
studying	*limud*	לימוד
syllabus	*tokhnit limudim*	תוכנית לימודים

■ TO LEAVE

לצאת
latset

Present (m.)		Present (f.)	
(s) *yotse*	יוצא	*yotset*	יוצאת
(pl) *yotsim*	יוצאים	*yotsot*	יוצאות

		Past		Future	
I	*ani*	*yatsati*	יצאתי	*etse*	אצא
you (m.)	*ata*	*yatsata*	יצאת	*tetse*	תצא
you (f.)	*at*	*yatsat*	יצאת	*titsi*	תצאי
he	*hu*	*yatsa*	יצא	*yetse*	יצא
she	*hi*	*yatsa*	יצאה	*tetse*	תצא
we	*anakhnu*	*yatsanu*	יצאנו	*netse*	נצא
you (pl.)	*atem*	*yatsatem*	יצאתם	*tetsu*	תצאו
they	*hem*	*yatsu*	יצאו	*yetsu*	יצאו

from...	*min, me...*	מן, מ...
from everything	*mikol hainyanim*	מכל העניינים
from here	*mikan*	מכאן
from him, us	*mimenu*	ממנו
from the building	*mehabinyan*	מהבניין
from the house	*mehabayit*	מהבית
from there	*misham*	משם
from you (m.)	*mimekha,*	ממך,
from you (f.)	*mimekh*	ממך
quickly	*maher*	מהר
slowly	*leat*	לאט
to...	*el...*	אל...
to...	*le...*	ל...
exit	*yetsiya*	יציאה
no exit	*eyn yetsiya*	אין יציאה
origin	*motsa*	מוצא
export	*yetsu*	יצוא
Where is the exit?	*eyfo yesh kan yetsiya?*	איפה יש כאן יציאה?
Where is the exit?	*eyfo hayetsiya?*	איפה היציאה?
outstanding	*yotse min haklal*	יוצא מן הכלל!

■ TO LIE (down...)

לשכב
lishkav

Present (m.)			Present (f.)	
(s)	shokhev	שוכב	shokhevet	שוכבת
(pl)	shokhvim	שוכבים	shokhvot	שוכבות

		Past		Future	
I	ani	shakhavti	שכבתי	eshkav	אשכב
you (m.)	ata	shakhavta	שכבת	tishkav	תשכב
you (f.)	at	shakhavt	שכבת	tishkevi	תשכבי
he	hu	shakhav	שכב	yishkav	ישכב
she	hi	shakhva	שכבה	tishkav	תשכב
we	anakhnu	shakhavnu	שכבנו	nishkav	נשכב
you (pl.)	atem	shakhavtem	שכבתם	tishkevu	תשכבו
they	hem	shakhvu	שכבו	yishkevu	ישכבו

to lie (down)...	lishkav...	לשכב...
for a while	ktsat	קצת
for a long time	harbe zman	הרבה זמן
alone	levad	לבד
in the corner	bapina	בפינה
in a drawer	bamegira	במגירה
in bed	bamita	במיטה
on the ground	al haadama	על האדמה
on the floor	al haritspa	על הרצפה
in the mud	babots	בבוץ
in the bath	baambatiya	באמבטיה

to be sick	*khole*	חולה
in the sun	*bashemesh*	בשמש
on the shore	*bakhof*	בחוף
in the shade	*batsel*	בצל
in the house	*babayit*	בבית
in the hospital	*babeit kholim*	בבית חולים
at night	*balaila*	בלילה
during the day	*bayom*	ביום
layer	*shikhva*	שיכבה
bed, lying down	*mishkav*	משכב
lying down, lying position	*shkhiva*	שכיבה
while lying down	*bishkhiva*	בשכיבה

■ TO LIVE (places)

לגור
lagur

Present (m.)			Present (f.)		
(s)	*gar*	גר	*gara*	גרה
(pl)	*garim*	גרים	*garot*	גרות

		Past		Future	
I	*ani*	*garti*	גרתי	*agur*	אגור
you (m.)	*ata*	*garta*	גרת	*tagur*	תגור
you (f.)	*at*	*gart*	גרת	*taguri*	תגורי
he	*hu*	*gar*	גר	*yagur*	יגור
she	*hi*	*gara*	גרה	*tagur*	תגור

we	*anakhnu*	*garnu*	גרנו	*nagur*	נגור
you (pl.)	*atem*	*gartem*	גרתם	*taguru*	תגורו
they	*hem*	*garu*	גרו	*yaguru*	יגורו

We lived in a 3-(4) room apartment.	*garnu badira shel shlosha (arbaa) khadarim*	גרנו בדירה של שלושה (ארבעה) חדרים.
to live...	*lagur...*	**לגור...**
in a hotel	*bemalon*	במלון
far away	*rakhok*	רחוק
in a good place (area)	*bemakom tov*	במקום טוב
in a new neighborhood	*beshkhuna khadasha*	בשכונה חדשה
in the center	*bamerkaz*	במרכז
in the city	*bair*	בעיר
in the same neighborhood	*beota shkhuna*	באותה שכונה
by the sea	*leyad hayam*	ליד הים
close to work	*leyad haavoda*	ליד העבודה
near by	*karov*	קרוב
on the first floor	*bekoma rishona*	בקומה ראשונה
on the second floor	*bekoma shniya*	בקומה שנייה
on the third floor	*bekoma shlishit*	בקומה שלישית
on the top floor	*bakoma haelyona*	בקומה העליונה
We want to live with our relatives (parents).	*anakhnu rotsim lagur yakhad im hakrovim (horim)*	אנחנו רוצים לגור יחד עם הקרובים (הורים).

■ TO LOOK FOR (private things, accessories)
■ TO SEARCH

לחפש
lekhapes

Present (m.)		Present (f.)	
(s) *mekhapes*	מחפש	*mekhapeset*	מחפשת
(pl) *mekhapsim*	מחפשים	*mekhapsot*	מחפשות

		Past		Future	
I	*ani*	*khipasti*	חפשתי	*akhapes*	אחפש
you (m.)	*ata*	*khipasta*	חפשת	*tekhapes*	תחפש
you (f.)	*at*	*khipast*	חפשת	*tekhapsi*	תחפשי
he	*hu*	*khipes*	חפש	*yekhapes*	יחפש
she	*hi*	*khipsa*	חפשה	*tekhapes*	תחפש
we	*anakhnu*	*khipasnu*	חפשנו	*nekhapes*	נחפש
you (pl.)	*atem*	*khipastem*	חפשתם	*tekhapsu*	תחפשו
they	*hem*	*khipsu*	חפשו	*yekhapsu*	יחפשו

I'm looking for...	*ani mekhapes...*	**...אני מחפש**
a hotel	*malon*	מלון
a room	*kheder*	חדר
a taxi	*monit*	מונית
a doctor	*rofe*	רופא
search	*khipus*	**חיפוש**
the Internet	*beinternet*	באינטרנט
search for...	*khipusim akharei...*	**...חיפושים אחרי**
suitable work	*haavoda*	העבודה
	hamat"ima	המתאימה
a bank	*bank*	בנק

a bus stop	*takhanat otobus*	תחנת אוטובוס
a grocery store	*makolet*	מכולת
medical help/ assistance	*ezra refuit*	עזרה רפואית
something suitable	*mashehu mat"im*	משהו מתאים
supermarket	*supermarket*	סופרמרקט
this person	*habenadam haze*	הבן אדם הזה
I've been looking for him for years.	*khipasti akharav shanim*	חפשתי אחריו שנים.
Are you looking for a cinema?	*ata mekhapes kolnoa?*	אתה מחפש קולנוע?
Did you look for him?	*khipasta oto?*	חפשת אותו?
What are you looking for?	*ma ata mekhapes?*	מה אתה מחפש?
Where is...?	*eyfo nimtsa...?*	איפה נמצא...?

■ TO LOSE

לאבד
leabed

		Present (m.)		Present (f.)	
(s)		*meabed*	מאבד	*meabedet*	מאבדת
(pl)		*meabdim*	מאבדים	*meabdot*	מאבדות

		Past		Future	
I	*ani*	*ibadti*	אבדתי	*eabed*	אאבד
you (m.)	*ata*	*ibadta*	אבדת	*teabed*	תאבד
you (f.)	*at*	*ibadt*	אבדת	*teabdi*	תאבדי
he	*hu*	*ibed*	אבד	*yeabed*	יאבד
she	*hi*	*ibda*	אבדה	*teabed*	תאבד
we	*anakhnu*	*ibadnu*	אבדנו	*neabed*	נאבד
you (pl.)	*atem*	*ibadtem*	אבדתם	*teabdu*	תאבדו
they	*hem*	*ibdu*	אבדו	*yeabdu*	יאבדו

to lose...   *leabed...*   **...לאבד**

to lose...	leabed...	
a/the checkbook	*pinkas chekim*	פנקס צ׳קים
a/the credit card	*kartis ashray*	כרטיס אשראי
a/the documents/ papers	*mismakhim*	מסמכים
the luggage	*mit"an*	מטען
money	*kesef*	כסף
my group	*et hakvutsa sheli*	את הקבוצה שלי
a/the passport	*darkon*	דרכון
a/the suitcase	*mizvada*	מזוודה

Don't lose this address.	*al teabed et haktovet hazot*	אל תאבד את הכתובת הזאת.
Don't lose your mind.	*al teabed et harosh*	אל תאבד את הראש.
all is lost	*hakol avud*	הכל אבוד
I lost everything.	*hakol avad li, ibadti et hakol*	הכל אבד לי, איבדתי את הכל.
I lost my notepad, wallet	*avad li pinkas, arnak*	אבד לי פנקס, ארנק
a difficult loss	*aveda kasha*	אבדה קשה
lost	*avud*	אבוד
suicide	*hitabdut*	התאבדות
We haven't lost hope.	*od lo avda tikvateynu*	עוד לא אבדה תקוותינו.

■ TO LOVE

לאהוב
leehov

	Present (m.)		**Present (f.)**	
(s)	*ohev*	אוהב	*ohevet*	אוהבת
(pl)	*ohavim*	אוהבים	*ohavot*	אוהבות

		Past		**Future**	
I	*ani*	*ahavti*	אהבתי	*ohav*	אוהב
you (m.)	*ata*	*ahavta*	אהבת	*tohav*	תאהב
you (f.)	*at*	*ahavt*	אהבת	*tohavi*	תאהבי
he	*hu*	*ahav*	אהב	*yohav*	יאהב
she	*hi*	*ahava*	אהבה	*tohav*	תאהב
we	*anakhnu*	*ahavnu*	אהבנו	*nohav*	נאהב
you (pl.)	*atem*	*ahavtem*	אהבתם	*tohavu*	תאהבו
they	*hem*	*ahavu*	אהבו	*yohavu*	יאהבו

love	*ahava*	אהבה
lover	*meahev*	מאהב
beloved	*ahuv*	אהוב
in love with...	*meuhav be...*	מאוהב ב...
fell in love	*hitahev*	התאהב

■ TO LOWER (adj.)

להוריד
lehorid

Present (m.)			Present (f.)	
(s)	*morid*	מוריד	*morida*	מורידה
(pl)	*moridim*	מורידים	*moridot*	מורידות

		Past		Future	
I	*ani*	*horadti*	הורדתי	*orid*	אוריד
you (m.)	*ata*	*horadta*	הורדת	*torid*	תוריד
you (f.)	*at*	*horadt*	הורדת	*toridi*	תורידי
he	*hu*	*horid*	הוריד	*yorid*	יוריד
she	*hi*	*horida*	הורידה	*torid*	תוריד
we	*anakhnu*	*horadnu*	הורדנו	*norid*	נוריד
you (pl.)	*atem*	*horadtem*	הורדתם	*toridu*	תורידו
they	*hem*	*horidu*	הורידו	*yoridu*	יורידו

carefully	*bizhirut*	בזהירות
down	*lemata*	למטה
from above	*milemala*	מלמעלה
take ... off of him	*lehorid mimenu*	להוריד ממנו
to the floor	*al haritspa*	על הרצפה
to the ground	*al hakarka*	על הקרקע
one by one	*ekhad ekhad*	אחד אחד
quickly	*maher*	מהר
slowly	*leat*	לאט
decrease, unloading	*horada*	הורדה
decrease	*yerida*	ירידה
in the exchange rate	*beshaar hamatbea*	בשער המטבע

■ TO MEET

להפגש
lehipagesh

Present (m.)			Present (f.)	
(s)	*nifgash*	נפגש	*nifgeshet*	נפגשת
(pl)	*nifgashim*	נפגשים	*nifgashot*	נפגשות

		Past		Future	
I	*ani*	*nifgashti*	נפגשתי	*epagesh*	אפגש
you (f.)	*ata*	*nifgashta*	נפגשת	*tipagesh*	תפגש
you (m.)	*at*	*nifgasht*	נפגשת	*tipagshi*	תפגשי
he	*hu*	*nifgash*	נפגש	*yipagesh*	יפגש
she	*hi*	*nifgesha*	נפגשה	*tipagesh*	תפגש
we	*anakhnu*	*nifgashnu*	נפגשנו	*nipagesh*	נפגש
you (pl.)	*atem*	*nifgashtem*	נפגשתם	*tipagshu*	תפגשו
they	*hem*	*nifgeshu*	נפגשו	*yipagshu*	יפגשו

with...	*im...*	**עם...**
a/the travel agent	*sokhen nesiyot*	סוכן נסיעות
the host	*hameareyakh*	המארח
a/the tour guide	*madrikh tiyulim*	מדריך טיולים
in a place we'll arrange	*bemakom shenikba*	במקום שנקבע
in another...	*beod...*	**בעוד...**
half an hour	*hatsi shaa*	חצי שעה
an hour	*shaa*	שעה
at (time)	*beshaa*	**בשעה**
12 o'clock exactly	*shteimesre bediyuk*	12 בדיוק
an appointment with...	*pgisha im...*	פגישה עם...

to meet	*lifgosh*	לפגוש
meeting	*mifgash*	מפגש

■ TO OPEN (objects)
liftoakh

לפתוח

Present (m.)			**Present (f.)**	
(s)	*poteyakh*	פותח	*potakhat*	פותחת
(pl)	*potkhim*	פותחים	*potkhot*	פותחות

		Past		**Future**	
I	*ani*	*patakhti*	פתחתי	*eftakh*	אפתח
you (m.)	*ata*	*patakhta*	פתחת	*tiftakh*	תפתח
you (f.)	*at*	*patakht*	פתחת	*tiftekhi*	תפתחי
he	*hu*	*patakh*	פתח	*yiftakh*	יפתח
she	*hi*	*patkha*	פתחה	*tiftakh*	תפתח
we	*anakhnu*	*patakhnu*	פתחנו	*niftakh*	נפתח
you (pl.)	*atem*	*patakhtem*	פתחתם	*tiftekhu*	תפתחו
they	*hem*	*patkhu*	פתחו	*yiftekhu*	יפתחו

at the opening	*baptikha*	בפתיחה
by chance	*beakray*	באקראי
entrance	*petakh*	פתח
key	*mafteyakh*	מפתח
now it's open	*akshav ze patuakh*	עכשיו זה פתוח
on purpose	*bekhavana*	בכוונה
open	*patuakh*	פתוח

an opener	*potkhan*	פותחן
opening	*ptikha*	פתיחה
please open	*tiftakh bevakasha*	תפתח בבקשה
the opening of...	*ptikhat...*	**פתיחת...**
an exhibition	*taarukha*	תערוכה
the book fair	*yerid hasfarim*	יריד הספרים
the office	*hamisrad*	המשרד
the bathing season	*onat harakhatsa*	עונת הרחצה
to open...	*liftoakh...*	**לפתוח...**
a conversation	*besikha*	בשיחה
an investigation	*bakhakira*	בחקירה
legal proceedings	*bahalikhim*	בהליכים
	mishpatiim	משפטיים
When does it open?	*matay ze niftakh*	?מתי זה נפתח

■ TO PAY (payments)

לשלם
leshalem

	Present (m.)		Present (f.)	
(s)	*meshalem*	משלם	*meshalemet*	משלמת
(pl)	*meshalmim*	משלמים	*meshalmot*	משלמות

		Past		Future	
I	*ani*	*shilamti*	שלמתי	*ashalem*	אשלם
you (m.)	*ata*	*shilamta*	שלמת	*teshalem*	תשלם
you (f.)	*at*	*shilamt*	שלמת	*teshalmi*	תשלמי
he	*hu*	*shilem*	שלם	*yeshalem*	ישלם

she	hi	*shilma*	שלמה	*teshalem*	תשלם
we	anakhnu	*shilamnu*	שלמנו	*neshalem*	נשלם
you (pl.)	atem	*shilamtem*	שלמתם	*teshalmu*	תשלמו
they	hem	*shilmu*	שלמו	*yeshalmu*	ישלמו

How much do I pay?	*kama ani meshalem?*	כמה אני משלם?
I pay by check.	*ani meshalem bachek*	אני משלם בצ'ק.
I paid the full amount.	*shilamti et mlo hakesef*	שלמתי את מלוא הכסף.
Is it possible to pay in installments?	*efshar leshalem betashlumim*	אפשר לשלם בתשלומים?
It's already been paid for!	*shulam kvar*	שולם כבר!
Pay at the register.	*shalem bakupa*	שלם בקופה.
payment	*tashlum*	תשלום
you paid cash	*shilamta bemezuman*	שלמת במזומן
You'll pay for this!	*ata od teshalem al kakh!*	אתה עוד תשלם על כך!

■ TO PARTICIPATE
■ TO SHARE

להשתתף
lehishtatef

Present (m.)   Present (f.)

	Present (m.)		Present (f.)	
(s)	*mishtatef*	משתתף	*mishtatefet*	משתתפת
(pl)	*mishtatfim*	משתתפים	*mishtatfot*	משתתפות

Past   Future

	Past		Future	
I	*hishtatafti*	השתתפתי	*eshtatef*	אשתתף
you (m.)	*hishtatafta*	השתתפת	*tishtatef*	תשתתף
you (f.)	*hishtataft*	השתתפת	*tishtatfi*	תשתתפי
he	*hishtatef*	השתתף	*yishtatef*	ישתתף
she	*hishtatfa*	השתתפה	*tishtatef*	תשתתף
we	*hishtatafnu*	השתתפנו	*nishtatef*	נשתתף
you (pl.)	*hishtataftem*	השתתפתם	*tishtatfu*	תשתתפו
they	*hishtatfu*	השתתפו	*yishtatfu*	ישתתפו

at a game	*bemiskhak*	במשחק
at a card game	*bemiskhak klafim*	במשחק קלפים
in the discussion	*badiyun*	בדיון
at work	*baavoda*	בעבודה
in this matter	*bainyan haze*	בעניין הזה
in the expenses	*bahotsaot*	בהוצאות
my condolences	*betsaar*	בצער
on participate during the trip	*betiyul*	בטיול

■ TO PHONE
■ TO RING UP

לטלפן
letalfen

	Present (m.)		Present (f.)	
(s)	*metalfen*	מטלפן	*metalfenet*	מטלפנת
(pl)	*metalfenim*	מטלפנים	*metalfenot*	מטלפנות

		Past		Future	
I	*ani*	*tilfanti*	טלפנתי	*atalfen*	אטלפן
you (m.)	*ata*	*tilfanta*	טלפנת	*tetalfen*	תטלפן
you (f.)	*at*	*tilfant*	טלפנת	*tetalfeni*	תטלפני
he	*hu*	*tilfen*	טלפן	*yitalfen*	יטלפן
she	*hi*	*tilfena*	טלפנה	*titalfen*	תטלפן
we	*anakhnu*	*tilfannu*	טלפנו	*netalfen*	נטלפן
you (pl.)	*atem*	*tilfantem*	טלפנתם	*tetalfenu*	תטלפנו
they	*hem*	*tilfenu*	טלפנו	*yetalfenu*	יטלפנו

■ TO PREFER

להעדיף
lehaadif

	Present (m.)		Present (f.)	
(s)	*maadif*	מעדיף	*maadifa*	מעדיפה
(pl)	*maadifim*	מעדיפים	*maadifot*	מעדיפות

		Past		Future	
I	*ani*	*heedafti*	העדפתי	*aadif*	אעדיף
you (m.)	*ata*	*heedafta*	העדפת	*taadif*	תעדיף
you (f.)	*at*	*heedaft*	העדפת	*taadifi*	תעדיפי
he	*hu*	*heedif*	העדיף	*yaadif*	יעדיף
she	*hi*	*heedifa*	העדיפה	*taadif*	תעדיף
we	*anakhnu*	*heedafnu*	העדפנו	*naadif*	נעדיף
you (pl.)	*atem*	*heedaftem*	העדפתם	*taadifu*	תעדיפו
they	*hem*	*heedifu*	העדיפו	*yaadifu*	יעדיפו

dairy	*khalavi*	חלבי
fish	*dagim*	דגים
meat	*basar*	בשר
red wine	**ya**in adom	יין אדום
to eat outside	*leekhol bakhuts*	לאכול בחוץ
to fly...	*latus...*	**לטוס...**
by charter	*becharter*	בצ'רטר
with El-Al airlines	*bekhevrat El-Al*	בחברת אל על...
in the no smoking section	*belo meashnim*	בלא מעשנים
to rent a room	*liskor kheder*	לשכור חדר

■ TO PROMISE (tickets for..., promises)

להבטיח
lehavtiyakh

Present (m.)			Present (f.)	
(s)	*mavtiyakh*	מבטיח	*mavtikha*	מבטיחה
(pl)	*mavtikhim*	מבטיחים	*mavtikhot*	מבטיחות

		Past		Future	
I	*ani*	*hevtakhti*	הבטחתי	*avtiyakh*	אבטיח
you (m.)	*ata*	*hevtakhta*	הבטחת	*tavtiyakh*	תבטיח
you (f.)	*at*	*hevtakht*	הבטחת	*tavtikhi*	תבטיחי
he	*hu*	*hevtiyakh*	הבטיח	*yavtiyakh*	יבטיח
she	*hi*	*hevtikha*	הבטיחה	*tavtiyakh*	תבטיח
we	*anakhnu*	*hevtakhnu*	הבטחנו	*navtiyakh*	נבטיח
you (pl.)	*atem*	*hevtakhtem*	הבטחתם	*tavtikhu*	תבטיחו
they	*hem*	*hevtikhu*	הבטיחו	*yavtikhu*	יבטיחו

a nice vacation	*khufsha neima*	חופשה נעימה
a room in a hotel	*kheder bemalon*	חדר במלון
excellent service	*shirut meule*	שירות מעולה
to lie in the sun	*lehishtazef*	להשתזף
to arrange everything	*lesader hakol*	לסדר הכל
to be careful	*lehizaher*	להיזהר
to come back (return)...	*lakhzor...*	לחזור...
by 7 o'clock	*besheva*	בשבע
the day after tomorrow	*mokhrotaim*	מחרתיים
today	*hayom*	היום
tomorrow	*makhar*	מחר

to go...	*lalekhet*	...ללכת
to the beach	*layam*	לים
on a trip	*letiul*	לטיול
to order tickets	*lehazmin kartisim*	**להזמין כרטיסים**
for the bus	*leotobus*	לאוטובוס
for the flight	*letisa*	לטיסה
for the performance	*lehatsaga*	להצגה
for the theater	*leteatron*	לתאטרון
for the train	*lerakevet*	לרכבת
to take care of...	*lishmor al...*	**לשמור על...**
yourself	*atsmekha*	עצמך
himself	*atsmo*	עצמו
herself	*atsma*	עצמה

■ TO READ (books, letters, emails...)
■ TO CALL

לקרוא
likro

	Present (m.)		Present (f.)	
(s)	*kore*	קורא	*koret*	קוראת
(pl)	*korim*	קוראים	*korot*	קוראות

		Past		Future	
I	*ani*	*karati*	קראתי	*ekra*	אקרא
you (m.)	*ata*	*karata*	קראת	*tikra*	תקרא
you (f.)	*at*	*karat*	קראת	*tikrei*	תקראי
he	*hu*	*kara*	קרא	*yikra*	יקרא
she	*hi*	*kar"a*	קראה	*tikra*	תקרא

we	*anakhnu*	*karanu*	קראנו	*nikra*	נקרא
you (pl.)	*atem*	*karatem*	קראתם	*tikreu*	תקראו
they	*hem*	*kar"u*	קראו	*yikreu*	יקראו

call him	*tikra lo*	תקרא לו
I want to read...	*ani rotse likro*	**אני רוצה לקרוא...**
the article	*et hamaamar*	את המאמר
the book	*et hasefer*	את הספר
the letter	*et hamikhtav*	את המכתב
the newspaper	*et haiton*	את העתון
Is there anything to read?	*yesh mashehu likro?*	יש משהו לקרוא?
What are you reading?	*ma ata kore?*	מה אתה קורא?
What's your name?	*eykh korim lekha?*	איך קוראים לך?
My name is Danny.	*shmi dani*	שמי דני.
call a doctor	*tikra lerofe*	תקרא לרופא
reading	*kria*	קריאה
it's called...	*ze nikra...*	זה נקרא...
I called you.	*karati lekha*	קראתי לך.

■ TO RECEIVE
■ TO GET

לקבל
lekabel

	Present (m.)		Present (f.)	
(s)	*mekabel*	מקבל	*mekabelet*	מקבלת
(pl)	*mekablim*	מקבלים	*mekablot*	מקבלות

		Past		Future	
I	*ani*	*kibalti*	קבלתי	*akabel*	אקבל
you (m.)	*ata*	*kibalta*	קבלת	*tekabel*	תקבל
you (f.)	*at*	*kibalt*	קבלת	*tekabli*	תקבלי
he	*hu*	*kibel*	קבל	*yekabel*	יקבל
she	*hi*	*kibla*	קבלה	*tekabel*	תקבל
we	*anakhnu*	*kibalnu*	קבלנו	*nekabel*	נקבל
you (pl.)	*atem*	*kibaltem*	קבלתם	*tekablu*	תקבלו
they	*hem*	*kiblu*	קבלו	*yekablu*	יקבלו

to get, receive...	*lekabel*	**לקבל...**
a bag	*tik*	תיק
financial assistance, contributions	*ezra kaspit, trumot*	עזרה כספית, תרומות
help	*ezra*	עזרה
lift, cargo	*mit"an*	מטען
a loan	*halvaa*	הלוואה
papers, certificates	*teudot*	תעודות
a salary	*maskoret*	משכורת
a suitcase, suitcases	*mizvada, mizvadot*	מזוודה, מזוודות

accepted (m.) (f.)	*mekubal, mekubelet*	מקובל, מקובלת
Got what he deserved.	*kibel et ma shemagia lo*	קבל את מה שמגיע לו.
reaching a decision	*kabalat hakhlata*	קבלת החלטה
receipt	*kabala*	קבלה
reception	*kabalat panim*	קבלת פנים

■ TO REMAIN (places)
■ TO STAY

להשאר
lehishaer

	Present (m.)		Present (f.)	
(s)	*nish"ar*	נשאר	*nisheret*	נשארת
(pl)	*nisharim*	נשארים	*nisharot*	נשארות

		Past		Future	
I	*ani*	*nish"arti*	נשארתי	*ashaer*	אשאר
you (m.)	*ata*	*nish"arta*	נשארת	*tishaer*	תישאר
you (f.)	*at*	*nish"art*	נשארת	*tish"ari*	תישארי
he	*hu*	*nish"ar*	נשאר	*yishaer*	ישאר
she	*hi*	*nish"ara*	נשארה	*tishaer*	תישאר
we	*anakhnu*	*nish"arnu*	נשארנו	*nishaer*	נישאר
you (pl.)	*atem*	*nish"artem*	נשארתם	*tish"aru*	תישארו
they	*hem*	*nish"aru*	נשארו	*yish"aru*	ישארו

to stay...	*lehish"aer...*	**...להשאר**
at the airport	*basde hateufa*	בשדה התעופה
at the hotel	*bamalon*	במלון

at work	*baavoda*	בעבודה
on the bus	*baotobus*	באוטובוס
in the house	*babayt*	בבית
at the office	*bamisrad*	במשרד
at the store	*bakhanut*	בחנות
inside	*bifnim*	בפנים
outside	*bakhuts*	בחוץ
with friends	*im hakhaverim*	עם החברים
with the children	*im hayeladim*	עם הילדים
with the family	*im hamishpakha*	עם המשפחה
with the husband	*im habaal*	עם הבעל
with the parents	*im hahorim*	עם ההורים
with the wife	*im haisha*	עם האישה
Don't stay here!	*al tishaer kan*	אל תישאר כאן!
I was left on my own.	*nish"arti levad*	נשארתי לבד.
A little is left.	*nish"ar ktsat*	נשאר קצת.
Nothing is left.	*lo nish"ar klum*	לא נשאר כלום.

■ TO REMEMBER

לזכור
lizkor

	Present (m.)			Present (f.)	
(s)	*zokher*	זוכר	*zokheret*	זוכרת	
(pl)	*zokhrim*	זוכרים	*zokhrot*	זוכרות	

		Past		Future	
I	*ani*	*zakharti*	זכרתי	*ezkor*	אזכור
you (m.)	*ata*	*zakharta*	זכרת	*tizkor*	תזכור
you (f.)	*at*	*zakhart*	זכרת	*tizkeri*	תזכרי
he	*hu*	*zakhar*	זכר	*yizkor*	יזכור
she	*hi*	*zakhra*	זכרה	*tizkor*	תזכור
we	*anakhnu*	*zakharnu*	זכרנו	*nizkor*	נזכור
you (pl.)	*atem*	*zakhartem*	זכרתם	*tizkeru*	תזכרו
they	*hem*	*zakhru*	זכרו	*yizkeru*	יזכרו

memory	*zikaron*	זכרון
these memories	*hazikhronot haele*	הזכרונות האלה
I don't remember.	*eyneni zokher*	אינני זוכר.
Do you remember?	*ata zokher?*	אתה זוכר?
I'll remember (what you did).	*ezkor lekha*	אזכור לך.

■ TO RETURN (public places, objects)
■ TO GO BACK

לחזור
lakhzor

Present (m.)			Present (f.)	
(s)	khoz**er**	חוזר	khoz**er**et	חוזרת
(pl)	khozr**im**	חוזרים	khozr**ot**	חוזרות

		Past		Future	
I	ani	khaz**ar**ti	חזרתי	akhz**or**	אחזור
you (m.)	ata	khaz**ar**ta	חזרת	takhz**or**	תחזור
you (f.)	at	khaz**ar**t	חזרת	takhz**eri**	תחזרי
he	hu	khaz**ar**	חזר	yakhz**or**	יחזור
she	hi	khaz**ra**	חזרה	takhz**or**	תחזור
we	anakhnu	khaz**ar**nu	חזרנו	nakhz**or**	נחזור
you (pl.)	atem	khaz**ar**tem	חזרתם	takhz**eru**	תחזרו
they	hem	khaz**ru**	חזרו	yakhz**eru**	יחזרו

from...	*min, me...*	...מן, מ
to...	*el...*	...אל
to...	*le...*	...ל
to the hotel	*lamal**on***	למלון
to the airport	*lenam**al** teufa*	לנמל תעופה
to the station	*latakh**ana***	לתחנה
to the train station	*letakh**anat** rakevet*	לתחנת רכבת
from a trip	*mitiy**ul***	מטיול
from a dinner	*mearukh**at** erev*	מארוחת ערב
from lunch	*mearukh**at** tsohoraim*	מארוחת צהריים
from breakfast	*mearukh**at** boker*	מארוחת בוקר

from a restaurant	*mimis"ada*	ממסעדה
from a discotheque	*midiscotek*	מדיסקוטק
from a club	*mimoadon*	ממועדון
from the beach	*mikhof hayam*	מחוף הים
from the army	*mehatsava*	מהצבא
from the movie	*mehaseret*	מהסרט
from the store	*mekhanut*	מחנות
from the clinic	*mikupat kholim*	מקופת חולים
to return home	*lakhzor habayta*	לחזור הביתה
to return	*lakhzor bekhazara*	לחזור בחזרה
tired	*ayef*	עייף
satisfied	*merutse*	מרוצה
hopeless, in despair	*meyuash*	מיואש
	(meyueshet)	(מיואשת)
rehearsal, review	*khazara*	חזרה
period, cycle	*makhzor*	מחזור
He changed his mind.	*hu khazar bo*	הוא חזר בו
	mehakavana hazot	מהכוונה הזאת.
please return	*takhzor bevakasha*	תחזור בבקשה

■ TO RETURN (something)

להחזיר
lehakhzir

Present (m.)		Present (f.)	
(s)	*makhzir* מחזיר	*makhzira*	מחזירה
(pl)	*makhzirim* מחזירים	*makhzirot*	מחזירות

		Past		Future	
I	*ani*	*hekhzarti*	החזרתי	*akhzir*	אחזיר
you (m.)	*ata*	*hekhzarta*	החזרת	*takhzir*	תחזיר
you (f.)	*at*	*hekhzart*	החזרת	*takhziri*	תחזירי
he	*hu*	*hekhzir*	החזיר	*yakhzir*	יחזיר
she	*hi*	*hekhzira*	החזירה	*takhzir*	תחזיר
we	*anakhnu*	*hekhzarnu*	החזרנו	*nakhzir*	נחזיר
you (pl.)	*atem*	*hekhzartem*	החזרתם	*takhziru*	תחזירו
they	*hem*	*hekhziru*	החזירו	*yakhziru*	יחזירו

my change	*et haodef sheli*	את העודף של
immediately	*miyad*	מיד
in a while	*beod zman ma*	בעוד זמן מה
in the afternoon	*akharey hatsohoraim*	אחרי הצהריים
in the evening	*baerev*	בערב
in the morning	*baboker*	בבוקר
after	*akharey*	אחרי
after this	*akharey ze*	אחרי זה
at noon	*betsohoraim*	בצהריים
next month	*bakhodesh haba*	בחודש הבא
next year	*bashana habaa*	בשנה הבאה

on time	*bazman, bamoed*	בזמן, במועד
the day after tomorrow	*mokhrotaim*	מחרתים
the day before yesterday	*shilshom*	שלשום
today	*hayom*	היום
tomorrow	*makhar*	מחר
yesterday	*etmol*	אתמול
I returned it.	*hekhzarti oto*	החזרתי אותו.
When will you return the book to me?	*matay takhzir li et hasefer?*	מתי תחזיר לי את הספר?
next week	*beshavua haba*	בשבוע הבא

■ TO SEE (what... & how...)

לראות
lir"ot

	Present (m.)		Present (f.)	
(s)	*roe*	רואה	*roa*	רואה
(pl)	*roim*	רואים	*root*	רואות

		Past		Future	
I	*ani*	*raiti*	ראיתי	*er"e*	אראה
you (m.)	*ata*	*raita*	ראית	*tir"e*	תראה
you (f.)	*at*	*rait*	ראית	*tir"i*	תראי
he	*hu*	**raa**	ראה	*yir"e*	יראה
she	*hi*	*raata*	ראתה	*tir"e*	תראה
we	*anakhnu*	*rainu*	ראינו	*nir"e*	נראה
you (pl.)	*atem*	*raitem*	ראיתם	*tir"u*	תראו
they	*hem*	*rau*	ראו	*yir"u*	יראו

clearly	bivhirut	בבהירות
everything	et hakol	את הכל
perfectly well	metsuyan	מצוין
good, well	tov	טוב
grocery	makolet	מכולת
hardly	bekoshi	בקושי
in the distance	bemerkhak	במרחק
next to...	karov el	קרוב אל...
next to, near...	leyad	ליד...
nothing	shum davar	שום דבר
store	khanut	חנות
the bus stop	takhanat otobus	תחנת אוטובוס
the corner	et hapina	את הפינה
the crossroad junction	et hatsomet	את הצומת
the house	et habayt	את הבית
the way, the road	et haderekh	את הדרך
this	et ze	את זה
this place	et hamakom haze	את המקום הזה
sight	mar"e	מראה
mirror	mar"a	מראה
visibility	reut	ראות
vision, view	reiya	ראיה
interview	raayon	ראיון
seems	nir"e	נראה
suitable	rauy	ראוי
is pessimistic	roe shkhorot	רואה שחורות
sees what the future holds	roe et hanolad	רואה את הנולד

accountant	*roe kheshbon*	רואה חשבון
see you later!	*lehitraot*	להתראות

■ TO SELL (home equipment)

למכור
limkor

Present (m.)

(s)	*mokher*	מוכר
(pl)	*mokhrim*	מוכרים

Present (f.)

mokheret	מוכרת
mokhrot	מוכרות

Past / Future

I	*ani*	*makharti*	מכרתי	*emkor*	אמכור
you (m.)	*ata*	*makharta*	מכרת	*timkor*	תמכור
you (f.)	*at*	*makhart*	מכרת	*timkeri*	תמכרי
he	*hu*	*makhar*	מכר	*yimkor*	ימכור
she	*hi*	*makhra*	מכרה	*timkor*	תמכור
we	*anakhnu*	*makharnu*	מכרנו	*nimkor*	נמכור
you (pl.)	*atem*	*makhartem*	מכרתם	*timkeru*	תמכרו
they	*hem*	*makhru*	מכרו	*yimkeru*	ימכרו

Where do they sell...? *eyfo mokhrim...?* **?...איפה מוכרים**

electrical appliances	*makhshirey khashmal*	מכשירי חשמל
refrigerators	*mekarerim*	מקררים
washing machines	*mekhonot kvisa*	מכונות כביסה
televisions	*televiziyot*	טלוויזיות
ovens	*tanurey afiya*	תנורי אפיה

air-conditioners	*mazganim*	מזגנים
fans	*meavrerim*	מאווררים
furniture:	*rehitey bayit:*	**רהיטי בית:**
bedroom set	*khadar shena*	חדר שינה
inbuilt closet	*aron kir*	ארון קיר
bed	*mita*	מיטה
mattress	*mizron*	מזרון
living room set	*salon*	סלון
snack bar	*miznon*	מזנון
bookcase	*konenit sfarim*	כוננית ספרים
armchair(s)	*kursa*	כורסא
	(kursaot)	(כורסאות)
chair(s)	*kise (kisaot)*	כסא (כסאות)
piano	*psanter*	פסנתר
table(s)	*shulkhan*	שולחן
	(shulkhanot)	(שולחנות)
clothing	*bgadim*	בגדים
sale	*mkhira*	מכירה
salesman	*mokher*	מוכר
has been, was sold	*nimkar*	נמכר
addicted to...	*makhur le...*	...מכור ל

■ TO SIT (places to sit on..., at...)

לשבת
lashevet

Present (m.)		Present (f.)	
(s) *yoshev*	יושב	*yoshevet*	יושבת
(pl) *yoshvim*	יושבים	*yoshvot*	יושבות

		Past		Future	
I	*ani*	*yashavti*	ישבתי	*eshev*	אשב
you (m.)	*ata*	*yashavta*	ישבת	*teshev*	תשב
you (f.)	*at*	*yashavt*	ישבת	*teshvi*	תשבי
he	*hu*	*yashav*	ישב	*yeshev*	ישב
she	*hi*	*yashva*	ישבה	*teshev*	תשב
we	*anakhnu*	*yashavnu*	ישבנו	*neshev*	נשב
you (pl.)	*atem*	*yashavtem*	ישבתם	*tishvu*	תשבו
they	*hem*	*yashvu*	ישבו	*yishvu*	ישבו

was sitting in the...	*yashav be...*	ישב ב...
seat	*makom yeshiva*	מקום ישיבה
chair	*kise*	כיסא
armchair	*kursa*	כורסא
lesson, class	*shiur*	שיעור
corner	*pina*	פינה
middle	*emtsa*	אמצע
first row	*shura rishona*	שורה ראשונה
was waiting with expectation for	*tsipiya le*	ציפיה ל...
was sitting quietly	*sheket*	שקט

was sitting on the side	*yashav betsad*	ישב בצד
sat on...	*yashav al...*	**ישב על...**
the chair	*hakise*	הכיסא
the floor	*haritspa*	הרצפה
the rug	*hashatiyakh*	השטיח
sat by the shore	*hakhof*	ישב על החוף
at...	*ba...*	**ב...**
the entrance	*knisa*	כניסה
the cafe	*kafe*	קפה
the restaurant	*mis"ada*	מסעדה
meeting	*yeshiva*	ישיבה
in the room	*kheder*	בחדר
seating	*yeshiva*	ישיבה
rural settlement	*moshav*	מושב
resident	*toshav*	תושב
settlement	*yeshuv*	ישוב
rear end	*yashvan*	ישבן
settled, inhabited, populated	*meyushav*	מיושב

■ TO SLEEP (bedroom)

לשון
lishon

Present (m.)			Present (f.)	
(s)	*yashen*	ישן	*yeshena*	ישנה
(pl)	*yeshenim*	ישנים	*yeshenot*	ישנות

		Past		Future	
I	*ani*	*yashanti*	ישנתי	*eshan*	אשן
you (m.)	*ata*	*yashanta*	ישנת	*tishan*	תישן
you (f.)	*at*	*yashant*	ישנת	*tishni*	תישני
he	*hu*	*yashan*	ישן	*yishan*	יישן
she	*hi*	*yashna*	ישנה	*tishan*	תישן
we	*anakhnu*	*yashanu*	ישנו	*nishan*	נישן
you (pl.)	*atem*	*yashantem*	ישנתם	*tishnu*	תישנו
they	*hem*	*yashnu*	ישנו	*yishnu*	יישנו

on...	*al...*	על...
the bed	*hamita*	המיטה
under..	*mitakhat la...*	מתחת ל...
the blanket	*smikha*	שמיכה
with...	*im...*	עם...
pillowcase(s)	*tsipa (tsipot)*	ציפה (ציפות)
pillow	*karit...*	כרית...
dirty .(f)	*melukhlekhet*	מלוכלכת
clean (f)	*nekiya*	נקיה
new (f)	*khadasha*	חדשה
old (f)	*yeshana*	ישנה

go to sleep late	*lalekhet lishon meukhar*	ללכת לישון מאוחר
go to sleep early	*lalekhet lishon mukdam*	ללכת לישון מוקדם
all night	*kol halayla*	כל הלילה
in piece	*besheket*	בשקט
from the evening through	*mehaerev*	מהערב
until the morning	*ad haboker*	עד הבוקר
with eyes open	*beeynaim pkukhot*	בעיניים פקוחות
all the way	*kol haderekh*	כל הדרך
all the time	*kol hazman*	כל הזמן
the lesson whole	*kol hashiur*	כל השיעור
sleep	*shena*	שינה
good night	*layla tov*	לילה טוב
sweet dreams	*khalomot metukim*	חלומות מתוקים

■ TO SMOKE

לעשן
leashen

Present (m.)

(s)	*meashen*	מעשן
(pl)	*meashnim*	מעשנים

Present (f.)

meashenet	מעשנת
meashnot	מעשנות

Past

I	*ani*	*ishanti*	עשנתי
you (m.)	*ata*	*ishanta*	עשנת
you (f.)	*at*	*ishant*	עשנת
he	*hu*	*ishen*	עשן
she	*hi*	*ishna*	עשנה
we	*anakhnu*	*ishanu*	עשנו
you (pl.)	*atem*	*ishantem*	עשנתם
they	*hem*	*ishnu*	עשנו

Future

eashen	אעשן
teashen	תעשן
teashni	תעשני
yeashen	יעשן
teashen	תעשן
neashen	נעשן
teashnu	תעשנו
yeashnu	יעשנו

you smoke a lot	*ata meashen harbe*	אתה מעשן הרבה
three packs a day	*shalosh khafisot beyom*	שלוש חפיסות ביום
smoking is not healthy	*ishun ze lo bari*	עישון זה לא בריא
smokes like a chimney	*meashen kmo katar*	מעשן כמו קטר
smoke	*ashan*	עשן
smoked fish	*dag meushan*	דג מעושן

■ TO SPEND TIME
■ TO GO OUT

לבלות
levalot

	Present (m.)		Present (f.)	
(s)	*mevale*	מבלה	*mevala*	מבלה
(pl)	*mevalim*	מבלים	*mevalot*	מבלות

		Past		Future	
I	*ani*	*biliti*	ביליתי	*avale*	אבלה
you (m.)	*ata*	*bilita*	בילית	*tevale*	תבלה
you (f.)	*at*	*bilit*	בילית	*tevali*	תבלי
he	*hu*	*bila*	בילה	*yevale*	יבלה
she	*hi*	*bilta*	בילתה	*tevale*	תבלה
we	*anakhnu*	*bilinu*	בילינו	*nevale*	נבלה
you (pl.)	*atem*	*bilitem*	ביליתם	*tevalu*	תבלו
they	*hem*	*bilu*	בילו	*yevalu*	יבלו

we spent...	*anakhnu bilinu...*	**אנחנו בילינו...**
all day...	*kol hayom...*	כל היום...
at the beach	*al sfat hayam*	על שפת הים
at the sea	*bayam*	בים
together	*beyakhad*	ביחד
with our friends	*im hakhaverim*	עם החברים
at our friends' place	*etsel hakhaverim*	אצל החברים
a great evening...	*erev nehedar...*	**ערב נהדר...**
at the theater	*bateatron*	בתאטרון
at the party	*bamesiba*	במסיבה

at a discotheque	*bediskotek*	בדיסקוטק
I spent my time...	*biliti*	**ביליתי**
at the restaurant	*bamis"ada*	במסעדה
in bed	*bamita*	במיטה
in front of the T.V.	*mul hatelevizia*	מול הטלוויזיה
Where can we go	**ey**fo efshar	איפה אפשר
for a good time?	*latset levalot?*	לצאת לבלות?
We want to have	*anakhau rotsim*	אנחנו רוצים
a good time.	*levalot*	לבלות.

■ TO STAND (position)

לעמוד
laamod

	Present (m.)		Present (f.)	
(s)	omed	עומד	omedet	עומדת
(pl)	omdim	עומדים	omdot	עומדות

		Past		Future	
I	ani	amadti	עמדתי	aamod	אעמוד
you (m.)	ata	amadta	עמדת	taamod	תעמוד
you (f.)	at	amadt	עמדת	taamdi	תעמדי
he	hu	amad	עמד	yaamod	יעמוד
she	hi	amda	עמדה	taamod	תעמוד
we	anakhnu	amadnu	עמדנו	naamod	נעמוד
you (pl.)	atem	amadtem	עמדתם	taamdu	תעמדו
they	hem	amdu	עמדו	yaamdu	יעמדו

to stand...	*laamod*	**...לעמוד**
behind...	*akharey*	...אחרי
in front of, before...	*lifney*	...לפני
in front of me	*lefanay*	לפניי
in front of you (m.)	*lefaneykha*	לפניך
in front of you (f.)	*lefanaikh*	לפניך
in front of him	*lefanav*	לפניו
in front of her	*lefaneya*	לפניה
in front of us	*lefaneynu*	לפנינו
in front of you (pl.)	*lifneykhem*	לפניכם
in front of them	*lifneyhem*	לפניהם
stood in front of me	*amad lefanay*	עמד לפניי
stood on guard	*amad al hamishmar*	עמד על המשמר
attention!	*amod dom*	!עמוד דום
stood...	*amad...*	**...עמד**
opposite	*mul*	מול
next to	*leyad*	ליד
outside	*bakhuts*	בחוץ
inside	*bifnim*	בפנים
on the side	*betsad*	בצד
in line	*bator*	בתור
passed the test	*amad bamivkhan*	עמד במבחן
kept his promise	*amad behavtakhato*	עמד בהבטחתו
stood still	*neemad*	נעמד
stand, position	*emda*	עמדה
his position is clear	*emdato brura*	עמדתו ברורה
wealthy (f.)	*amida*	עמידה

standing up	*beamida*	בעמידה
page, column	*amud*	עמוד

■ TO STOP

לעצור
laatsor

	Present (m.)		Present (f.)	
(s)	*otser*	עוצר	*otseret*	עוצרת
(pl)	*otsrim*	עוצרים	*otsrot*	עוצרות

		Past		Future	
I	*ani*	*atsarti*	עצרתי	*aatsor*	אעצור
you (m.)	*ata*	*atsarta*	עצרת	*taatsor*	תעצור
you (f.)	*at*	*atsart*	עצרת	*taatsri*	תעצרי
he	*hu*	*atsar*	עצר	*yaatsor*	יעצור
she	*hi*	*atsra*	עצרה	*taatsor*	תעצור
we	*anakhnu*	*atsarnu*	עצרנו	*naatsor*	נעצור
you (pl.)	*atem*	*atsartem*	עצרתם	*taatsru*	תעצרו
they	*hem*	*atsru*	עצרו	*yaatsru*	יעצרו

immediately	*bamakom*	במקום
at the red light	*beor adom*	באור אדום
at a (road) crossing	*lifney maavar khatsaya*	לפני מעבר חצייה
at the bus stop	*batakhana*	בתחנה
for ten minutes	*leeser dakot*	לעשר דקות
for half an hour	*lekhatsi shaa*	לחצי שעה

once	*paam akhat*	פעם אחת
twice	*paamaim*	פעמיים
3 times	*shalosh peamim*	שלוש פעמים
during the drive	*bemeshekh hanesiya*	במשך הנסיעה

■ TO TAKE (from..., in order...)

לקחת
lakakhat

Present (m.)		Present (f.)	
(s) *lokeyakh*	לוקח	*lokakhat*	לוקחת
(pl) *lokkhim*	לוקחים	*lokkhot*	לוקחות

		Past		Future	
I	*ani*	*lakakhti*	לקחתי	*ekakh*	אקח
you (m.)	*ata*	*lakakhta*	לקחת	*tikakh*	תקח
you (f.)	*at*	*lakakht*	לקחת	*tikkhi*	תקחי
he	*hu*	*lakhakh*	לקח	*yikakh*	יקח
she	*hi*	*lakkha*	לקחה	*tikakh*	תקח
we	*anakhnu*	*lakakhnu*	לקחנו	*nikakh*	נקח
you (pl.)	*atem*	*lakakhtem*	לקחתם	*tikkhu*	תקחו
they	*hem*	*lakkhu*	לקחו	*yikkhu*	יקחו

change	**odef**	עודף
...ticket	*kartis...*	**כרטיס...**
travel	*nesiya*	נסיעה
plane	*tisa*	טיסה
train	*rakevet*	רכבת

bus	**o**tobus	אוטובוס
suitcase	mizvad**a**	מזוודה
key	mafteyakh	מפתח
money	k**e**sef	כסף
from where?	mi**ey**fo	מאיפה?
from me	mimeni	ממני
from you (m.)	mimkha	ממך
from you (f.)	mimekh	ממך
from him	mim**e**nu	ממנו
from her	mim**e**na	ממנה
from us	mim**e**nu	ממנו
from you (pl.)	mik**e**m	מכם
from them	mih**e**m	מהם
a little, bit	ktsat	קצת
a lot	harb**e**	הרבה
easy	bekal**u**t	בקלות
with difficulty, hardly	bek**o**shi	בקושי
forever	leolam	לעולם
for a certain anount of time	lezman mesuy**a**m	לזמן מסוים
for a few minutes	lekhama dak**o**t	לכמה דקות
separately	benifrad	בנפרד
together	be**ya**khad	ביחד
back	khazar**a**	חזרה
quietly	besheket	בשקט
in order (to)	bematara	במטרה
in order (to)	bekhavana	בכוונה
unintentionally	bel**o** kavana	בלא כוונה

■ TO TELL (adj.)
■ TO SAY (adj.)

להגיד
lehagid
לומר
lomar

Present (m.) / Present (f.)

		Present (m.)		Present (f.)	
(s)		*omer*	אומר	*omeret*	אומרת
(pl)		*omrim*	אומרים	*omrot*	אומרות

Past / Future

		Past		Future	
I	ani	*amarti*	אמרתי	*omar*	אומר
you (m.)	ata	*amarta*	אמרת	*tomar*	תאמר
you (f.)	at	*amart*	אמרת	*tomri*	תאמרי
he	hu	*amar*	אמר	*yomar*	יאמר
she	hi	*amra*	אמרה	*tomar*	תאמר
we	anakhnu	*amarnu*	אמרנו	*nomar*	נאמר
you (pl.)	atem	*amartem*	אמרתם	*tomru*	תאמרו
they	hem	*amru*	אמרו	*yomru*	יאמרו

			Future	
I	ani		*agid*	אגיד
you (m.)	ata		*tagid*	תגיד
you (f.)	at		*tagidi*	תגידי
he	hu	*past not used*	*yagid*	יגיד
she	hi		*tagid*	תגיד
we	anakhnu		*nagid*	נגיד
you (pl.)	atem		*tagidu*	תגידו
they	hem		*yagidu*	יגידו

to tell (say)...	lomar...	**לומר ...**
afterwards	akhar kakh	אחר כך
a lot	harbe	הרבה
not a lot	lo harbe	לא הרבה
correctly	nakhon	נכון
everything	hakol	הכל
not everything	lo hakol	לא הכל
in his name	bishmo	בשמו
in the beginning	behatkhala	בהתחלה
something	mashehu	משהו
that it isn't so	sheze lo nakhon	שזה לא נכון
the opposite	leheyfekh	להיפך
the truth	et haemet	את האמת
is supposed to be...	amur lihyot...	אמור להיות...
he was told...	neemar lo	נאמר לו
they say that...	omrim she...	אומרים ש...
This man says...	haadam haze omer...	האדם הזה אומר...
That woman told...	haisha hahi amra...	האישה ההיא אמרה...
is supposed to do...	amur laasot...	אמור לעשות...
a saying	amira	אמירה
legend, tale	agada	אגדה
let's say that...	nagid she...	נגיד ש...
tell me	tagid li	תגיד לי

■ TO TELL
■ TO CUT HAIR

לספר
lesaper

Present (m.)			Present (f.)	
(s)	*mesaper*	מספר	*mesaperet*	מספרת
(pl)	*mesaprim*	מספרים	*mesaprot*	מספרות

		Past		Future	
I	ani	*siparti*	ספרתי	*asaper*	אספר
you (m.)	ata	*siparta*	ספרת	*tesaper*	תספר
you (f.)	at	*sipart*	ספרת	*tesapri*	תספרי
he	hu	*siper*	ספר	*yesaper*	יספר
she	hi	*sipra*	ספרה	*tesaper*	תספר
we	anakhnu	*siparnu*	ספרנו	*nesaper*	נספר
you (pl.)	atem	*sipartem*	ספרתם	*tesapru*	תספרו
they	hem	*sipru*	ספרו	*yesapru*	יספרו

to tell...
lesaper...
לספר ...

everything	*et hakol*	את הכל
not everything	*lo hakol*	לא הכל
in detail	*bekhol hapratim*	בכל הפרטים
how was it?	*eykh ze haya?*	איך זה היה?
precisely	*bimeduyak*	במדויק
the truth	*et haemet*	את האמת
what happened	*ma shehaya*	מה שהיה
without going into detail	*belo lefaret*	בלא לפרט
story	*sipur*	סיפור

a fictitious story	*sipur baduy*	סיפור בדוי
is told	*mesupar*	מסופר
book	*sefer*	ספר
school book	*sefer limud*	ספר לימוד
writer	*sofer*	סופר
counting	*sfira*	ספירה
number	*mispar*	מספר
library	*sifriya*	ספריה
barber	*sapar*	ספר
to get a haircut	*lehistaper*	להסתפר

■ TO THINK (about...)

לחשוב
lakhshov

	Present (m.)		Present (f.)	
(s)	*khoshev*	חושב	*khoshevet*	חושבת
(pl)	*khoshvim*	חושבים	*khoshvot*	חושבות

		Past		Future	
I	*ani*	*khashavti*	חשבתי	*akhshov*	אחשוב
you (m.)	*ata*	*khashavta*	חשבת	*takhshov*	תחשוב
you (f.)	*at*	*khashavt*	חשבת	*takhshevi*	תחשבי
he	*hu*	*khashav*	חשב	*yakhshov*	יחשוב
she	*hi*	*khashva*	חשבה	*takhshov*	תחשוב
we	*anakhnu*	*khashavnu*	חשבנו	*nakhshov*	נחשוב
you (pl.)	*atem*	*khashavtem*	חשבתם	*takhshevu*	תחשבו
they	*hem*	*khashvu*	חשבו	*yakhshevu*	יחשבו

I thought...	*khashavti...*	**חשבתי...**
about	*al*	על
about you (m.)	*alekha*	עליך
about you (f.)	*alayikh*	עליך
about him	*alav*	עליו
about her	*aleha*	עליה
about us	*aleynu*	עלינו
about you (pl.)	*aleykhem*	עליכם
about you (f.pl.)	*aleyhem*	עליהם
about this idea	*al haraayon haze*	על הרעיון הזה
about all this	*al kol ze*	על כל זה
that...	*she...*	ש...
importance	*khashivut*	חשיבות
thought	*makhshava*	מחשבה
important	*khashuv*	חשוב
important that...	*khashuv she...*	חשוב ש...
we'll think about...	*nakhshov al...*	נחשוב על...
math, bill, account	*kheshbon*	חשבון
calculated	*mekhushav*	מחושב
calculation	*khishuv*	חישוב
considering...	*behitkhashev be...*	בהתחשב ב...
thinks ahead	*khoshev merosh*	חושב מראש

■ TO TRAVEL (places, transport)
■ TO GO
■ TO DRIVE

לנסוע
linsoa

Present (m.)			Present (f.)	
(s)	*nosea*	נוסע	*nosaat*	נוסעת
(pl)	*nos"im*	נוסעים	*nos"ot*	נוסעות

		Past		Future	
I	*ani*	*nasati*	נסעתי	*esa*	אסע
you (m.)	*ata*	*nasata*	נסעת	*tisa*	תסע
you (f.)	*at*	*nasat*	נסעת	*tis"i*	תסעי
he	*hu*	*nasa*	נסע	*yisa*	יסע
she	*hi*	*nasa*	נסעה	*tisa*	תסע
we	*anakhnu*	*nasanu*	נסענו	*nisa*	נסע
you (pl.)	*atem*	*nasatem*	נסעתם	*tis"u*	תסעו
they	*hem*	*nasu*	נסעו	*yis"u*	יסעו

from (the)...	*me, meha...*	...מ, מה
to where?	*leeyfo?*	?לאיפה
to...	*el...*	...אל
to...	*le, la...*	**...ל**
Israel	*israel*	ישראל
Jerusalem	*yerushalayim*	ירושלים
Tel Aviv	*tel aviv*	תל אביב
Haifa	*kheyfa*	חיפה
Be'er Sheva	*beersheva*	באר-שבע
Eilat	*eylat*	אילת

Western Wall	*el hakotel*	אל הכותל
	hamaaravi	המערבי
a/the mall	*kanyon*	קניון
at the...	*la...*	**...ל**
city	*ir*	עיר
center	*merkaz*	מרכז
supermarket	*supermarket*	סופרמרקט
police	*mishtara*	משטרה
hospital	*beyt kholim*	בית חולים
to relatives	*krovey mishpakha*	קרובי משפחה
to friends	*khaverim*	חברים
to beach	*yam*	ים
to the army	*tsava*	צבא
to look for...	*lekhapes...*	...לחפש
to study...	*lilmod...*	**...ללמוד**
medicine	*refua*	רפואה
engineering	*handasa*	הנדסה
to live	*likhyot*	לחיות
to see	*lir"ot*	לראות
to visit	*levaker*	לבקר
to meet...	*lifgosh*	**...לפגוש**
with him	*oto*	אותו
with her	*ota*	אותה
with them	*otam*	אותם
fast	*maher*	מהר
slow	*leat*	לאט
far	*rakhok*	רחוק
near by	*karov*	קרוב

in a/an...	*be...*	**...ב**
bus	**o**tobus	אוטובוס
number...	*mispar...*	מספר...
automobile	**o**to	אוטו
in...car	*bemekhonit...*	**...במכונית**
my	*sheli*	שלי
a new	*khadasha*	חדשה
a heavy	*kveda*	כבדה
on a truck	*bemasait*	במשאית
on a train	*berakevet*	ברכבת
in a plane	*bematos*	במטוס
on a...	*ba...*	**...ב**
ship	*sfina*	ספינה
road	*kvish*	כביש
intercity road	*kvish beynironi*	כביש בינעירוני
path, lane, way	*maslul*	מסלול
regular	*ragil*	רגיל
set	*kavua*	קבוע
passenger	*nosea*	נוסע
passengers	*nos"im*	נוסעים
trip	*nesia*	נסיעה
ride, transportation	*hasaa*	הסעה

■ TO WAIT (for...)   לחכות
lekhakot

Present (m.)			Present (f.)	
(s)	*mekhake*	מחכה	*mekhaka*	מחכה
(pl)	*mekhakim*	מחכים	*mekhakot*	מחכות

		Past		Future	
I	*ani*	*khikiti*	חכיתי	*akhake*	אחכה
you (m.)	*ata*	*khikita*	חכית	*tekhake*	תחכה
you (f.)	*at*	*khikit*	חכית	*tekhaki*	תחכי
he	*hu*	*khika*	חכה	*yekhake*	יחכה
she	*hi*	*khikta*	חכתה	*tekhake*	תחכה
we	*anakhnu*	*khikinu*	חכינו	*nekhake*	נחכה
you (pl.)	*atem*	*khikitem*	חכיתם	*tekhaku*	תחכו
they	*hem*	*khiku*	חכו	*yekhaku*	יחכו

to wait...	*lekhakot...*	‫...לחכות‬
for the train	*lerakevet*	לרכבת
for the bus	*leotobus*	לאוטובוס
for the flight	*latisa*	לטיסה
for an answer	*latshuva*	לתשובה
for the opening	*laptikha*	לפתיחה
for the closing	*lasgira*	לסגירה
for the beginning	*lahatkhala*	להתחלה
for the end	*lasof*	לסוף
in the queue	*bator*	בתור
by the table	*leyad hashulkhan*	ליד השולחן

on the beach	*al hakhof*	על החוף
for a long time	*harbe zman*	הרבה זמן
for support	*letmikha*	לתמיכה
from the morning	*mehaboker*	מהבוקר
till evening	*ad haerev*	עד הערב
in vain	*lashav*	לשוא
I waited for you	*khikiti lekha*	חכיתי לך
Wait a minute!	*khake rega*	חכה רגע!
waited for nothing	*khika lashav*	חכה לשוא

■ TO WANT (activities, places)

לרצות
lirtsot

	Present (m.)		Present (f.)	
(s)	*rotse*	רוצה	*rotsa*	רוצה
(pl)	*rotsim*	רוצים	*rotsot*	רוצות

		Past		Future	
I	*ani*	*ratsiti*	רציתי	*ertse*	ארצה
you (m.)	*ata*	*ratsita*	רצית	*tirtse*	תרצה
you (f.)	*at*	*ratsit*	רצית	*tirtsi*	תרצי
he	*hu*	*ratsa*	רצה	*yirtse*	ירצה
she	*hi*	*ratsta*	רצתה	*tirtse*	תרצה
we	*anakhnu*	*ratsinu*	רצינו	*nirtse*	נרצה
you (pl.)	*atem*	*ratsitem*	רציתם	*tirtsu*	תרצו
they	*hem*	*ratsu*	רצו	*yirtsu*	ירצו

I want...	*ani rotse...*	**...אני רוצה**
to find out	*levarer*	לברר
to do	*laasot*	לעשות
to eat	*leekhol*	לאכול
to meet with	*lehipagesh im*	להפגש עם
to drink	*lishtot*	לשתות
to request, to ask for	*levakesh*	לבקש
to go to the toilet	*lesherutim*	לשרותים
to sit	*lashevet*	לשבת
to think	*lakhshov*	לחשוב
to rest	*lanuakh*	לנוח
to lie down a little while	*lishkav ktsat*	לשכב קצת
to sleep	*lishon*	לשון
money	*kesef*	כסף
an apartment	*dira*	דירה
to go...	*lalekhet...*	**...ללכת**
there	*lesham*	לשם
to his place	*elav*	אליו
to the agency	*lasokhnut*	לסוכנות
to the bank	*labank*	לבנק
to the doctor	*larofe*	לרופא
to the hospital	*labeyt kholim*	לבית חולים
to the medical center	*lekupat kholim*	לקופת חולים
to the toilet	*lesherutim*	לשרותים
to your place	*elekha, elaikh (f.)*	אליך

to say...	*lomar...*	**...לומר**
to you (m.)	*lekha*	לך
to you (f.)	*lakh*	לך
that...	*she...*	ש...
I have	*ani tsarikh*	אני צריך
to see...	*lir"ot*	**...לראות**
this	*et ze*	את זה
my relatives	*et hakrovim sheli*	את הקרובים שלי
the apartment	*et hadira*	את הדירה
this clerk	*et hapakid haze*	את הפקיד הזה
this form	*et hatofes haze*	את הטופס הזה
this place	*et hamakom haze*	את המקום הזה
this man	*et haish haze*	את האיש הזה
you (m.)	*otkha*	אותך
you (f.)	*otakh*	אותך

■ TO WASH (toilet accessories, kitchen equipment)

לשטוף
lishtof

Present (m.)			Present (f.)	
(s)	*shotef*	שוטף	*shotefet*	שוטפת
(pl)	*shotfim*	שוטפים	*shotfot*	שוטפות

		Past		Future	
I	*ani*	*shatafti*	שטפתי	*eshtof*	אשטוף
you (m.)	*ata*	*shatafta*	שטפת	*tishtof*	תשטוף
you (f.)	*at*	*shataft*	שטפת	*tishtefi*	תשטפי
he	*hu*	*shataf*	שטף	*yishtof*	ישטוף
she	*hi*	*shatfa*	שטפה	*tishtof*	תשטוף
we	*anakhnu*	*shatafnu*	שטפנו	*nishtof*	נשטוף
you (pl.)	*atem*	*shataftem*	שטפתם	*tishtefu*	תשטפו
they	*hem*	*shatfu*	שטפו	*yishtefu*	ישטפו

wash the car	*lishtof et haoto*	לשטוף את האוטו
washed away in the rain	*nishtaf bageshem*	נשטף בגשם

■ TO WASH
■ TO BATHE

לרחוץ
lirkhots

Present (m.)			Present (f.)	
(s)	*rokhets*	רוחץ	*rokhetset*	רוחצת
(pl)	*rokhatsim*	רוחצים	*rokhatsot*	רוחצות

		Past		Future	
I	*ani*	*rakhatsti*	רחצתי	*erkhats*	ארחץ
you (m.)	*ata*	*rakhatsta*	רחצת	*tirkhats*	תרחץ
you (f.)*	*at*	*rakhatst*	רחצת	*tirkhetsi*	תרחצי
he	*hu*	*rakhats*	רחץ	*yirkhats*	ירחץ
she	*hi*	*rakhatsa*	רחצה	*tirkhats*	תרחץ
we	*anakhnu*	*rakhatsnu*	רחצנו	*nirkhats*	נרחץ
you (pl.)	*atem*	*rakhatstem*	רחצתם	*tirkhetsu*	תרחצו
they	*hem*	*rakhatsu*	רחצו	*yirkhetsu*	ירחצו

in hot water	*bemaim khamim*	במים חמים
with soap	*im sabon*	עם סבון
with a toothbrush	*bemivreshet shinaim*	במברשת שיניים
with a sponge	*besfog*	בספוג
with warm water	*bemaim poshrim*	במים פושרים
with cold water	*bemaim karim*	במים קרים
in the morning	*baboker*	בבוקר
hands	*yadaim*	ידיים
face	*panim*	פנים
feet	*raglaim*	רגליים

after going to the toilet — *akharey hasherutim* — אחרי השרותים

in the shower — *bamiklakhat* — במקלחת

under the faucet/tap — *takhat haberez* — תחת הברז

wash the dishes: — *tirkhats (tishtof) et hakelim* — **תרחץ (תשטוף) את הכלים...**

bowl (bowls) — *keara (kearot)* — קערה (קערות)

cup (cups) — *kos (kosot)* — כוס (כוסות)

cup (cups) — *sefel (sfalim)* — ספל (ספלים)

fork (forks) — *mazleg (mazlegot)* — מזלג (מזלגות)

frying pan (frying pans) — *makhvat (makhvatot)* — מחבת (מחבתות)

kettle(s) — *kumkum(im)* — קומקום (ים)

knife (knives) — *sakin (sakinim)* — סכין (סכינים)

pan(s) — *tavnit (tavniyot)* — תבנית (תבניות)

plate (plates) — *tsalakhat (tsalakhot)* — צלחת (צלחות)

pot (pots) — *sir (sirim)* — סיר (סירים)

small (wine) cups — *kosit (kosiyot)* — כוסית (כוסיות)

spoon (spoons) — *kaf (kapot)* — כף (כפות)

teaspoon (teaspoons) — *kapit (kapiyot)* — כפית (כפיות)

tray(s) — *magash(im)* — מגש (מגשים)

very clean — *naki naki* — נקי נקי

wipe with the towel — *lenagev bemagevet* — לנגב במגבת

to do the laundry — *lekhabes et hakvisa* — לכבס את הכביסה

take a shower/bath — *lehitrakhets* — להתרחץ

I took a shower/bath. — *hitrakhatsti* — התרחצתי.

You took a shower/bath. — *hitrakhatsta* — התרחצת.

■ TO WIN (games)

לנצח
lenatseyakh

Present (m.)		Present (f.)	
(s)	*menatseyakh*	מנצח	*menatsakhat*	מנצחת
(pl)	*menatskhim*	מנצחים	*menatskhot*	מנצחות

		Past		Future	
I	*ani*	*nitsakhti*	נצחתי	*anatseyakh*	אנצח
you (m.)	*ata*	*nitsakhta*	נצחת	*tenatseyakh*	תנצח
you (f.)	*at*	*nitsakht*	נצחת	*tenatskhi*	תנצחי
he	*hu*	*nitsakh*	נצח	*yenatseyakh*	ינצח
she	*hi*	*nitskha*	נצחה	*tenatseyakh*	תנצח
we	*anakhnu*	*nitsakhnu*	נצחנו	*nenatseyakh*	ננצח
you (pl.)	*atem*	*nitsakhtem*	נצחתם	*tenatskhu*	תנצחו
they	*hem*	*nitskhu*	נצחו	*yenatskhu*	ינצחו

the games:	*bemiskhak*	במשחק:
basketball	*kadursal*	כדורסל
football	*kaduregel*	כדורגל
golf	*golf*	גולף
card	*klafim*	קלפים
tennis	*tenis*	טניס
by...	*be*	ב...
jumping	*kfitsa...*	קפיצה
long jumping	*leorekh*	לאורך
high jumpung	*legova*	לגובה
the race	*meruts*	במרוץ

197

swimming	*skhiya*	שחיה
(to win) the bet	*hit"arvut*	התערבות

■ TO WRITE

לכתוב
likhtov

Present (m.)			Present (f.)	
(s)	*kotev*	כותב	*kotevet*	כותבת
(pl)	*kotvim*	כותבים	*kotvot*	כותבות

		Past		Future	
I	*ani*	*katavti*	כתבתי	*ekhtov*	אכתוב
you (m.)	*ata*	*katavta*	כתבת	*tikhtov*	תכתוב
you (f.)	*at*	*katavt*	כתבת	*tikhtevi*	תכתבי
he	*hu*	*katav*	כתב	*yikhtov*	יכתוב
she	*hi*	*katva*	כתבה	*tikhtov*	תכתוב
we	*anakhnu*	*katavnu*	כתבנו	*nikhtov*	נכתוב
you (pl.)	*atem*	*katavtem*	כתבתם	*tikhtevu*	תכתבו
they	*hem*	*katvu*	כתבו	*yikhtevu*	יכתבו

letter	*mikhtav*	מכתב
e-mail	**email**	אי מאיל
note	*petek*	פתק
address	*ktovet*	כתובת
article	*katava*	כתבה
the...	*et ha...*	**את ה...**
proposal	*hatsaa*	הצעה

business plan	tokhnit iskit	תוכנית עסקית
curriculum vitae	korot haim	קורות חיים
abstract	taktsir	תקציר
correspondence	hitkatvut	התכתבות
journalist	katav	כתב
dictated	mukhtav	מוכתב
dictation	takhtiv	תכתיב
handwriting	ktav yad	כתב יד
in printed letters	beotiyot dfus	באותיות דפוס
is written	katuv	כתוב
our correspondent	kataveynu	כתבינו
newspaper, magazine	ktav et	כתב עת
quickly	maher	מהר
to dictate	lehaktiv	להכתיב
was written	nikhtav	נכתב
write clearly	likhtov barur	לכתוב ברור

■ TO WORK (professions, on..., with..., in...)   לעבוד
laavod

Present (m.)		Present (f.)	
(s)	*oved* — עובד	*ovedet* — עובדת
(pl)	*ovdim* — עובדים	*ovdot* — עובדות

		Past		Future	
I	*ani*	*avadti*	עבדתי	*eevod*	אעבוד
you (m.)	*ata*	*avadta*	עבדת	*taavod*	תעבוד
you (f.)	*at*	*avadt*	עבדת	*taavdi*	תעבדי
he	*hu*	*avad*	עבד	*yaavod*	יעבוד
she	*hi*	*avda*	עבדה	*taavod*	תעבוד
we	*anakhnu*	*avadnu*	עבדנו	*naavod*	נעבוד
you (pl.)	*atem*	*avadtem*	עבדתם	*taavdu*	תעבדו
they	*hem*	*avdu*	עבדו	*yaavdu*	יעבדו

to work...	*laavod...*	**...לעבוד**
in order to...	*kdey, bishvil...*	...כדי, בשביל
on...	*al...*	...על
with...	*im...*	...עם
with, in...	*be...*	ב...
I worked...	*avadti...*	**...עבדתי**
at school	*beveit sefer*	בבית ספר
in a hospital	*beveit kholim*	בבית חולים
in a lab	*bemaabada*	במעבדה
in an office	*bemisrad*	במשרד
in education	*bekhinukh*	בחינוך

work (works)	avoda (avodot)	עבודה (עבודו)
suitable work	avoda mat"ima	עבודה מתאימה
at work	baavoda	בעבודה
from work	mehaavoda	מהעבודה
processing	ibud	עיבוד
processed	meubad	מעובד
employer (m.) (f.)	oved, ovedet	עובד, עובדת
I am...	ani...	**אני...**
a chemist	khimai	כימאי
a clerk (m.) (f.)	pakid, pkida	פקיד, פקידה
a doctor (m.) (f.)	rofe, rof"a	רופא, רופאה
a driver	nahag	נהג
an electrician	khashmalay	חשמלאי
an engineer	mehandes	מהנדס
a lecturer (m.) (f.)	martse, martsa	מרצה, מרצה
a mathematician	matematikai	מתמטיקאי
a nurse	akhot	אחות
a physicist	fizikai	פיסיקאי
a researcher	khoker	חוקר
a scientist	mad"an	מדען
a teacher (m.) (f.)	more, mora	מורה, מורה
a technician	tekhnai	טכנאי
a student (m., f.)	student, studentit	סטודנט, סטודנטית
a waiter	meltsar	מלצר
a waitress	meltsarit	מלצרית
a business man	ish asakim	איש עסקים

■ A

a bit	ktsat	קצת
a bit more	ktsat yoter;	קצת יותר;
	od ktsat	עוד קצת
a bit of patience	ktsat savlanut	קצת סבלנות
a certain type	sug mesuyam	סוג מסוים
a growing gap	paar holekh vegadel	פער הולך וגדל
a lucky person	bar mazal	בר מזל
a mess	esek bish	עסק ביש
a pause	pesek zman	פסק זמן
a pity	khaval	חבל
a pity that he...	khaval shehu...	...חבל שהוא
a real character	masmer khazak	מסמר חזק
A real nightmare!	siyut, mamash siyut!	סיוט, ממש סיוט
a serious mistake	fashla retsinit	פשלה רצינית
a slap in the face	stirat lekhi	סטירת לחי
a waste of time	bizbuz zman	בזבוז זמן
about it	al kakh	על כך
About what?	al ma	?על מה
absolutely not	beferush lo	בפרוש לא
acceptable	maniyakh et hadaat	מניח את הדעת
actually	beetsem, lemaase	בעצם, למעשה
after...	akharey she...	...אחרי ש
after all	akharey hakol	אחרי הכל
after this	akharey ze	אחרי זה
afterwards	akhar kakh	אחר כך
all	kol	כל
allow me	harshe li	...הרשה לי

also	gam ken	גם כן
among other things	beyn hashaar;	בין השאר;
	beyn hayeter	בין הייתר
an eye for an eye	ain takhat ain	עין תחת עין
and even so	uvekhol zot	ובכל זאת
And how!	veod eykh!	ועוד איך
and more	veod	ועוד
and nothing else	veshum davar akher	ושום דבר אחר
and so	uvekhen	ובכן
And that's it!	vetu lo!	ותו לא!
And what not?	uma lo!	ומה לא
And what of it?	uma bekhakh	ומה בכך
another time	paam akheret	פעם אחרת
anything you want	kol ma sheata	כל מה שאתה
	rotse	רוצה
anyway	belav hakhi	בלווא הכי
apparently	kfi hanir"e	כפי הנראה
Are you coming? (m., f.)	ata ba,	אתה בא?
	at baa?	את באה?
Are you happy, content?	tov lekha	טוב לך?
Are you satisfied?	merutse, merutsa (f.)	מרוצה?
as...	kmo she...	כמו ש...
as a reaction	bitguva	בתגובה
as a... (in the position of)	betor...	בתור...
as if	keilu	כאילו
as long as	kol od	כל עוד
as needed	kfi shetsarikh	כפי שצריך

as you know (m.)	*kfi she ata yodea*	כפי שאתה יודע
as you please (m.)	*eykh sheata rotse*	איך שאתה רוצה
aside from that	*khuts mize*	חוץ מזה
at his strongest	*bimlo hakoakh*	במלוא הכח
at his fittest	*bimlo hakosher*	במלוא הכושר
at the head	*berosh*	בראש
Attention!	*hakshev!*	הקשב!
award	*tsalash*	צל"ש
Awful!	*nora!*	נורא!

■ B

barber	*sapar*	ספר
Bastard!	*mamzer*	ממזר
before	*kodem*	קודם
beginning	*hatkhala*	התחלה
Best wishes!	*kol tuv lekha*	כל טוב לך!
blooper	*fashla*	פשלה
boor	*bur*	בור
boring	*meshaamem*	משעמם
breakdown in communication	*ketser batikshoret*	קצר בתקשורת
burst out laughing	*parats bitskhok*	פרץ בצחוק
but	*aval*	אבל

■ C

Can...?	*haim...*	האם...?
Can you be relied upon?	*efshar lismokh aleykha (alaykh)*	אפשר לסמוך עליך?

carefully	bizhirut	בזהירות
certain aspect, particular part	tsad mesuyam	צד מסויים
certainly	behekhlet; behekhlet ken	בהחלט; בהחלט כן
certainly not	behekhlet lo	בהחלט לא
change it	teshane et ze	תשנה את זה
character	barnash	ברנש
come here	bo hena	בוא הנה
come on already	bo kvar; nu kvar	בוא כבר; נו כבר
Come on, you are kidding!	bekhayekha!	בחייך!
Come quickly!	bo maher!	בוא מהר
come tomorrow	tavo makhar	תבוא מחר
commotion	saarat rukhot	סערת רוחות
completely incidental	shuli legamre	שולי לגמרי
concerning which	benogea lekakh	בנוגע לכך
confusion, mix up	bilbul	בלבול
congratulations	kol hakavod	כל הכבוד
contradicts himself	soter et atsmo	סותר את עצמו
countdown	sfira leakhor	ספירה לאחור

◼ D

decision-making	kabalat hakhlata	קבלת החלטה
Definitely not!	beshum ofen	בשום אופן
desirable	ratsuy	רצוי
despite...	af she...; al af...	אף ש...; על אף...
disgusting	goal nefesh	גועל נפש

do me a favour	*taase li tova*	תעשה לי טובה
Do you care?	*ikhpat lekha*	איכפת לך?
Do you know?	*haim ata yodea*	האם אתה יודע?
Do you see him?	*roe oto?*	רואה אותו?
Does it matter for you?	*meshane lekha?*	משנה לך?
Don't be like that!	*al tih"ye kaze!*	אל תהיה כזה!
don't bother	*lo tsarikh*	לא צריך
Don't bother me!	*red mimeni!*	רד ממני!
Don't do that!	*al taase zot!*	אל תעשה זאת!
Don't forget!	*al tishkakh!*	אל תשכח!
Don't let it get to you!	*al tikakh lalev!*	אל תקח ללב!
Don't pay any attention!	*al tasim lev!*	אל תשים לב!
Don't take!	*al tikakh!*	אל תקח!
Don't worry!	*al tid"ag!*	אל תדאג!
Don't you dare.	*oy veavoy lekha*	אוי ואבוי לך.
during	*bemeshekh*	במשך

■ E

encountered difficulties	*nitkal bikshaim*	נתקל בקשיים
enlistment orders	*tsav giyus*	צו גיוס
Enough!	*day! khalas!*	די! חלס!
Enough already!	*day kvar!*	די כבר!
Enough! Go!	*day! lekh!*	די! לך!
Enter! Come in!	*yavo!*	יבוא!
even	*afilu*	אפילו
even though you did it	*afilu asita zot*	אפילו עשית זאת
Every dog has its day.	*torkha od yagia*	תורך עוד יגיע.

every single one, one by one	ekhad ekhad	אחד אחד
everyone	kol ekhad	כל אחד
everything	hakol	הכל
everything is clear here	po hakol barur	פה הכל ברור
everything is fine	hakol beseder	הכל בסדר
everything is OK	hakol beseder	הכל בסדר
exactly in the same situation	beoto matsav bediyuk	באותו מצב בדיוק
except for...	prat le...	פרט ל...
except for me	khuts mimeni	חוץ ממני
except for that (this)	prat lekhakh	פרט לכך
Excuse me! Pardon me!	slikha	סליחה
excuse me, please	slakh li bevakasha	סלח לי בבקשה
explicitly	beferush	בפרוש

■ F

finally	sof sof	סוף סוף
first and foremost	berosh uverishona	בראש ובראשונה
first of all	kodem kol; reshit kol	קודם כל; ראשית כל
firstly	berishona	בראשונה
fool	tipesh	טיפש
for all this	al kol panim	על כל פנים
for everything	al kol davar	על כל דבר
for it, for everything	al kakh	על כך
for some reason	mishum she...	משום ש...
for that reason	leshem kakh	לשם כך

forever	*vead bikhlal*	ועד בכלל
Forget it!	*tishkakh mize!*	תשכח מזה!
forgive me	*slakh li*	סלח לי
Forward!	*kadima!*	קדימה!

■ G

get it (him) for me	*tasig li oto*	תשיג לי אותו
Get out!	*hakhutsa!*	החוצה!
Get out of here!	*tse mikan*	צא מכאן!
Get up!	*kum!*	קום!
Get up already!	*kum kvar!*	קום כבר!
give it to me	*ten li oto*	תן לי אותו
gladly	*beratson*	ברצון
go already!	*lekh kvar*	לך כבר
God forbid!	*khas vekhalila!;*	;חס וחלילה
	khas veshalom!	חס ושלום
Good-bye!	*shalom lehitraot!*	שלום להתראות!
good morning	*boker tov*	בוקר טוב
got screwed	*nidfak*	נדפק
Great!	*shigaon! yesh!*	שגעון! יש!
great majority	*rov makhria*	רוב מכריע

■ H

hand in hand (together)	*yad beyad*	יד ביד
handsome (a hunk)	*khatikh*	חתיך
hard to know	*kashe ladaat*	קשה לדעת
hard to understand	*kashe lehavin*	קשה להבין

Have a nice time!	*bilui naim*	‏בלוי נעים!
He contradicts himself.	*yesh stirot bidvarav*	‏יש סתירות בדבריו.
he's still not in	*adain eyneno*	‏עדיין איננו
heavy burden	*netel kaved*	‏נטל כבד
Hello! Shalom!	*shalom!*	‏שלום!
here	*po*	‏פה
here and there	*po vesham*	‏פה ושם
hi!	*ahalan vesahalan!*	‏אהלן וסאהלן;
	ahalan!	‏אהלן!
hiding something	*mastir mashehu*	‏מסתיר משהו
honestly	*bekenut*	‏בכנות
Horrible!	*zvaa!*	‏זוועה!
How?	*eykh?*	‏איך?
How are you?	*ma itkha?*	‏מה איתך?
	ma nishma?	‏מה נשמע?
How do like it?	*eykh ze?*	‏איך זה?
humanity	*tselem enosh*	‏צלם אנוש
hypocrite!	*tsavua!*	‏צבוע!

■ I

I care a lot.	*ikhpat li meod*	‏איכפת לי מאוד
I didn't know.	*lo yadati*	‏לא ידעתי
I don't care.	*lo ikhpat li;*	‏לא איכפת לי;
	ze lo meziz li.	‏זה לא מזיז לי.
I don't feel like.	*eyn li kheshek*	‏אין לי חשק.
I don't have strength.	*eyn koakh*	‏אין כח.
I don't want to!	*lo rotse!*	‏לא רוצה!
I don't yet have...	*adain eyn li...*	‏עדיין אין לי...

I doubt…	yesh li safek	...יש לי ספק
I just didn't know what to do.	pashut lo yadati ma laasot	פשוט לא ידעתי מה לעשות.
I still don't know.	terem noda li	טרם נודע לי.
I want…	ani rotse	...אני רוצה
I want you to know.	ani rotse sheteda	אני רוצה שתדע.
I'll check it.	evdok zot	אבדוק זאת.
I'll gladly see you.	esmakh lir"ot otkha	אשמח לראות אותך.
I'll have to think about it.	etstarekh lakhshov al kakh	אצטרך לחשוב על כך.
I'll tear you apart!	ani afarek otkha!	אני אפרק אותך!
I'll tell you the truth.	agid lekha et haemet	אגיד לך את האמת.
I'll think about it.	eshkol zot	אשקול זאת.
I'm dead tired.	ani harug	אני הרוג.
I'm still waiting.	ani adain mekhake	אני עדיין מחכה.
Idiot! idiot	metumtam!, tumtum, tembel	מטומטם!, טומטום, טמבל
if not you…	lule ata…	...לולא אתה
if so	im kakh; im ken	אם כך; אם כן
if that's the way it is, then…	im kakh, az…	...אם כך אז
if that's the way you are…	im ata kakha…	...אם אתה ככה
immediately	miyad; teykhef umiyad	מיד; תיכף ומיד
Impossible!	lo yiktakhen	לא יתכן!

Impossible! Forbidden!	*i-efshar!*	!אי אפשר
in any case	*bekhol ofen;*	;בכל אופן
	beyn ko vakho;	;בין כה וכה
	mikol makom	מכל מקום
in general	*bikhlal*	בכלל
in his prime	*bemeytavo*	במיטבו
in light of...	*leor...*	...לאור
in order...	*bikhdey...*	...בכדי
in order...; for...	*kdey...*	...כדי
in order to...	*al mnat...*	...על מנת
in the beginning	*behatkhala*	בהתחלה
in the end...	*sofo shel davar*	סופו של דבר
	haya she...	...היה ש
in the fullest meaning	*bimlo muvan*	במלוא מובן
of the word	*hamila*	המילה
in the long run	*bitvakh arokh*	בטווח ארוך
in the same place	*beoto makom*	באותו מקום
in the same situation	*beoto matsav*	באותו מצב
in the short run	*bitvakh katsar*	בטווח קצר
incorrect	*lo nakhon*	לא נכון
indeed	*akhen*	אכן
indeed, truly	*omnam*	אמנם
innocent: not guilty	*khaf mipesha*	חף מפשע
irresponsibility	*khoser akhrayut*	חוסר אחראיות
Is it enough?	*yaspik lekha?*	?יספיק לך
Is it so hard for you?	*kol kakh kashe lekha?*	?כל כך קשה לך
Is it true/correct/right?	*ze nakhon?*	?זה נכון
Is this way to do it?	*kakh osim?*	?כך עושים

Isn't it true?	*haeyn ze nakhon?*	?האין זה נכון
it amazes me that...	*mafli oti she...*	...מפלאי אותי ש
it appears as if...	*haroshem hu she...*	...הרושם הוא ש
it can't be	*lo yakhol lihyot*	לא יכול להיות
it could be	*yakhol lihyot*	יכול להיות
it could have been	*yakhol haya lihyot*	יכול היה להיות
it depends	*ze talui*	זה תלוי
It doesn't interest me.	*lo meanyen oti*	.לא מעניין אותי
It doesn't make any difference.	*kvar lo meshane*	.כבר לא משנה
it doesn't matter	*lo meshane*	לא משנה
It doesn't suit you	*lo mat"im lekha*	לא מתאים לך
it is forbidden	*asur!*	אסור
it is over (finished)	*tam venishlam*	תם ונשלם
it is possible	*yetakhen*	יתכן
it is strange that...	*meshune she...*	...משונה ש
it isn't necessary	*eyn tsorekh*	אין צורך
It simply isn't succeeding, it is not suitable	*pashut lo holekh*	.פשוט לא הולך
it sounds good	*nishma tov*	נשמע טוב
It stinks here!	*masriyakh kan!*	!מסריח כאן
it turns out that...	*mistaber she...*	...מסתבר ש
it was hinted at that...	*nirmaz she...*	...נרמז ש
it won't help	*ze lo yaazor*	זה לא יעזור
it won't succeed	*ze lo yelekh*	זה לא ילך
it won't succeed this way	*kakha ze lo yelekh*	ככה זה לא ילך

It'll be OK	ih"ye beseder	.יהיה בסדר
it's awfully hot	kham nora	חם נורא
it's easy to think that...	kal lakhshov she...	...קל לחשוב ש
it's fact	uvda	עובדה
It's good that you said so.	tov sheamarta	.טוב שאמרת
it's good to know	tov ladaat	טוב לדעת
it's highly possible	yitakhen meod	יתכן מאוד
it's necessary...	ze hekhrekhi	...זה הכרחי
it's no wonder that...	lo pele she...	...לא פלא ש
it's not clear	lo barur	לא ברור
it's not OK	lo beseder	לא בסדר
It's not worth your while.	lo keday lekha	.לא כדי לך
It's not your business.	ze lo inyankha	.זה לא עניינך
it's senseless, there is no sense	eyn taam	אין טעם
it's too late; its too late already	kvar meukhar	כבר מאוחר
it's true that...	nakhon she...	...נכון ש
it's unlike you	lo dome lekha	לא דומה לך
it's worth it	lo shave	לא שווה
it's worthwhile	keday	כדאי

■ J

just a bit	tip tipa	טיפ-טיפה
just opened his mouth	rak patakh et hape	רק פתח את הפה
justice	tsedek	צדק

justly, rightly so	*betsedek*	בצדק

■ K

know	*da lekha*	דע לך

■ L

leave it (me...)	*azov*	עזוב
Leave it alone! forget it!	*azov et ze*	עזוב את זה
Leave me alone!	*azov oti!*	!עזוב אותי
let him go	*sheyelekh*	שילך
Let him go to hell! damn him	*sheyelekh leazazel*	!שילך לעזאזל
let it go	*taazov et ze*	תעזוב את זה
let me see	*ten li lir"ot*	תן לי לראות
let's do it	*bo naase*	בוא נעשה
Let's eat something.	*nokhal mashehu*	.נאכל משהו
Let's go!	*ya*la	יאלה
let's go	*nelekh; zaznu*	נלך; זזנו
let's hurry	*keday lehizdarez*	כדאי להזדרז
let's say that...	*nagid she...;* *nomar she...*	;...נגיד ש ...נאמר ש
let's suppose	*naniyakh*	נניח
Let's wind up the matter, come to an agreement	*nisgor inyan*	נסגור ענין
Liar!	*shakran*	!שקרן
like nothing	*kmo klum*	כמו כלום
Listen!	*tishma*	!תשמע

listen, you...	tishma khabub...	...תשמע חבוב
long ago	ze mikvar	זה מכבר
Look!	tir"e!	תראה!
Look at what we have here.	ree ma yesh kan	ראה מה יש כאן.
looking back on it	bediavad	בדיעבד

■ M

mainly, especially	beikar	בעיקר
manage somehow	tistader eykhshehu	תסתדר איכשהו
May I?	mutar?	מותר
mess	balagan	בלגן
mindlessly	bli rosh	בלי ראש
mockingly	belaag	בלעג
mood, bad mood	matsav ruakh	מצב רוח
more than anything	yoter mikol	יותר מכל
more than this	yoter mize	יותר מזה
more, still	od	עוד
moreover	yetira mikakh	יתירה מכך
most	rov	רוב
Most definitely not!	beshum panim vaofen	בשום פנים ואופן
most of the time	rov hazman	רוב הזמן
most people	rov haanashim	רוב האנשים
most probably	karov levaday	קרוב לוודאי
mouth	pe	פה
move aside!	zuz hatsida	זוז הצידה

■ N

necessary condition	*tnai bal yaavor*	תנאי בל יעבור
need to (have to)	*tsarikh*	צריך
never mind	*lo khashuv;*	לא חשוב;
	meyele	מילא
nevertheless	*bekhol zot*	בכל זאת
next	*hakarov*	הקרוב
no	*lo*	לא
no luck	*eyn mazal*	אין מזל
no matter, never mind	*eyn davar*	אין דבר
no one	*af ekhad*	אף אחד
...no one	*...et af ekhad*	...את אף אחד
no one wants	*af ekhad lo rotse*	אף אחד לא רוצה
no problem	*eyn shum baaya*	אין שום בעיה
No way!	*ma pit"om!*	מה פתאום!
No way!	*lo ba bekheshbon!*	לא בא בחשבון!
Nonsense!	*shtuyot!*	שטויות!
nonsense, lies	*bablat*	בבל"ט
not at all	*bikhlal lo*	בכלל לא
not certain	*lo batuakh*	לא בטוח
not connected, related	*lo kashur*	לא קשור
not everything	*lo hakol*	לא הכל
not exactly	*lo bediyuk*	לא בדיוק
not good	*lo tov*	לא טוב
not having a choice	*beleyt brera*	בלית ברירה
not in the mood	*eyn matsav ruakh*	אין מצב רוח
not long ago	*lo mikvar;*	לא מכבר;
	lo mizman	לא מזמן

Not really!	*lav davka*	לאו דווקא!
Not necessarily.		
not significant	*lo mashmauti*	לא משמעותי
not so much	*lo kol kakh*	לא כל כך
not that I'm	*lo sheani*	לא שאני
against it, but...	*mitnaged, aval...*	מתנגד, אבל...
not that!	*lo ze!*	לא זה
not the same thing	*lo oto davar*	לא אותו דבר
not there	*lo sham*	לא שם
not this way	*lo kakha*	לא ככה
not to	*lo bikhdey*	לא בכדי
not useful	*lo shimushi*	לא שמושי
not worthwhile for you	*lo keday lekha (m.)*	לא כדאי לך
not yet	*od lo*	עוד לא
nothing	*klum;*	כלום;
	shum davar	שום דבר
nothing new	*shum davar khadash*	שום דבר חדש
nothing can be done	*eyn ma laasot*	אין מה לעשות
nudnik, pest	*nudnik*	נודניק

■ O

OK, stop bugging me	*beseder, beseder*	בסדר בסדר
OK	*beseder*	בסדר
object to...	*kovel al...*	קובל על...
of course	*kamuvan*	כמובן
on condition that...	*betnay she...*	בתנאי ש...
on condition,	*al tnay*	על תנאי
on probation		

on purpose, purposely	*bekhavana*	בכוונה
on the basis of...	*al smakh...*	על סמך...
on the contrary	*adraba*	אדרבה
on time	*bamoed*	במועד
on what basis?	*al smakh ma?*	על סמך מה?
once	*paam; paam akhat*	פעם; פעם אחת
one of them	*ekhad mihem*	אחד מהם
one way or another	*eykh shehu;*	איך שהוא;
	kakh o akheret	כך או אחרת
opened his mouth	*patakh et hape*	פתח את הפה
	shelo	שלו
other	*akher*	אחר
other than this	*prat lekhakh*	פרט לכך

■ P

parallel to,	*bemakbil*	במקביל
at the same time		
particularly difficult	*kashe bim"yukhad*	קשה במיוחד
perfectly fine, OK	*beseder gamur*	בסדר גמור
perhaps	*ulay*	אולי
Pig!	*khazir!*	חזיר!
please	**ana**; *na*	אנא; נא
please (Arabic)	*tfadal*	תפדל
Please get up!	*kum bevakasha*	קום בבקשה
please listen	*na lehakshiv*	נא להקשיב
please move	*tazuz bevakasha*	תזוז בבקשה
please sit down	*na lashevet,*	נא לשבת,
	teshev bevakasha	תשב בבקשה

previously	*lifney khen*	לפני כן
prostitute, whore	*zona*	זונה
purposely	*bemitkaven*	במתכוון

■ Q

quick, alert, active	*zariz*	זריז
quiet!	*sheket*	שקט!

■ R

rabbi	*rav*	רב
Read it!	*kra et ze!*	קרא את זה!
really beautiful	*nora yafe*	נורא יפה
Really!	*bekhayay!*	בחיי!
Really?	*beemet?,*	באמת?,
	haomnam?	האמנם?
reception	*kabalat panim*	קבלת פנים
rely on me!	*smokh alay!*	סמוך עלי!
Right?, True?	*nakhon?*	נכון?
right here	*po bamakom*	פה במקום
Right now?	*kvar akhshav?*	כבר עכשיו?
run!	*ruts!*	רוץ!
Run quickly!	*ruts maher!*	רוץ מהר!

■ S

sad	*metsuvrakh*	מצוברח
satisfactory	*masbia ratson*	משביע רצון
say	*tagid*	תגיד
Savage! Wild thing!	*pere adam!*	פרא אדם!

seriously	*bekhol hartsinut*	בכל הרצינות
Seriously?	*birtsinut?*	ברצינות?
several	*akhadim*	אחדים
several times	*paamim akhadot*	פעמים אחדות
Sexy!	*khatikha*	חתיכה
Shall we continue?	*namshikh?*	נמשיך?
Shall we go?	*nelekh?*	נלך?
shortly	*bekitsur*	בקיצור
Shut up!	*shtok!*	שתוק!
Shut up already!	*shtok kvar!*	שתוק כבר!
side, part	*tsad*	צד
side by side	*tsad betsad*	צד בצד
silently	*bishtika*	בשתיקה
simple	*pashut*	פשוט
simply	*pshuto kimashmao*	פשוטו כמשמעו
Sit down! Sit!	*shev!*	שב!
Sit quietly!	*shev besheket!*	שב בשקט!
sit quietly	*teshev besheket*	תשב בשקט
slap, contradiction	*stira*	סתירה
slight bruise, scratch	*srita ktana*	שריטה קטנה
slight hesistation	*tsel shel hisus*	צל של היסוס
slowly	*beitiyut*	באיטיות
slowly, little by little	*leat leat*	לאט לאט
smoothly	*khad vekhalak*	חד וחלק
so-so	*kakha kakha*	ככה ככה
So how was it?	*nu eykh haya?*	נו איך היה?
so much	*kol kakh*	כל כך
something else	*mashehu akher*	משהו אחר

something strange	*mashehu muzar*	משהו מוזר
son of a bitch	*ben zona*	בן זונה
soon	*bekarov; teykhef*	בקרוב; תיכף
Speak up!	*daber!*	!דבר
Stand at attention!	*amod dom*	!עמוד דום
still, yet	*adain*	עדיין
still without change	*adain lelo shinuy*	עדיין ללא שינוי
Stop!	*atsor!*	!עצור
Stop it!	*tafsik*	!תפסיק
strange	*muzar*	מוזר
stuffy, suffocating	*makhnik*	מחניק
suddenly	*pit"om*	פתאום
suitable	*mat"im*	מתאים
supported a	*tsided betsad*	צידד בצד
certain party	*mesuyam*	מסויים
suspense movie	*seret metakh*	סרט מתח
Sweet heart!	*motek!*	!מותק

■ T

Take care of yourself!	*shmor al atsmekha*	!שמור על עצמך
tell me, please	*tagid bevakasha*	תגיד בבקשה
tensely	*bedrikhut*	בדריכות
thanks a lot	*toda raba*	תודה רבה
that is necessasry	*ze tsarikh*	זה צריך
that is to say...	*zot omeret...*	...זאת אומרת
that the way it is	*kakha ze*	ככה זה
that's a lie	*sheker*	!שקר

that's all I can do	ze kol ma sheani yakhol laasot	זה כל מה שאני יכול לעשות
that's boring	ze meshaamem	זה משעמם
That's enough for him.	dai lo beze (bekhakh).	די לו בזה (בכך).
that's enough	ze maspik	זה מספיק
that's final	vesof pasuk	וסוף פסוק
That's final!	nekuda!	נקודה!
that's foolish	ze tipshi	זה טפשי
that's good	ze tov	זה טוב
that's it	zehu ze	זהו זה
that's new to me	ze khadash bishvili	זה חדש בשבילי
that's nice	ze yafe	זה יפה
that's not enough	ze lo maspik	זה לא מספיק
that's not important	ze lo khashuv	זה לא חשוב
that's the main thing	ze haikar	זה העיקר
that's very important	ze khashuv meod	זה חשוב מאוד
that's what I thought	kakh khashavti	כך חשבתי
That's what you have to say?	ze ma sheyesh lekha lehagid?	זה מה שיש לך להגיד?
the best	hatov beyoter	הטוב ביותר
the main thing	haikar	העיקר
the masses	amkha	עמך
the meaning of it is that...	pesher hadavar she...	פשר הדבר ש...
the point is...	hanekuda hi...	הנקודה היא...
the result of...	poal yotse min... (shel)	פועל יוצא מן... (של...)

the source of the conflict	zera hamakhloket	זרע המחלוקת
the subject is closed	nigmar hainyan	נגמר העניין
the thing is that	kol hainyan hu she...	כל העניין הוא ש...
the thing most precious to me	hadavar hayakar bishvili	הדבר היקר בשבילי
there are all kinds	yesh vayesh	יש ויש
there is no choice	eyn brera	אין ברירה
there is no doubt	eyn shum safek	אין שום ספק
There is no doubt that...	eyn safek she...	אין ספק ש...
there is no reason	eyn shum siba	אין שום סיבה
there is no way	eyn shum efsharut	אין שום אפשרות
there is none	eyn	אין
There is nothing to talk about...	eyn al ma ledaber	אין על מה לדבר
There is something in it.	yesh beze mashehu	יש בזה משהו
There is something strange...	yesh mashehu muzar	יש משהו מוזר
therefore	al ken; i-lekakh	על כן; אי לכך
they	hem, hen (f.)	הם, הן
this	ze	זה
this is on condition that	kol ze betnay she...	כל זה בתנאי ש...
this way	kakh	כך
time after time	paam akharey paam	פעם אחרי פעם
to act	lif"ol	לפעול
to be	lihyot	להיות
to close the gap	lisgor et hapaar	לסגור את הפער
to do	laasot	לעשות

to help out	*latet katef*	לתת כתף
to judge by its merits	*lishkol kol davar legufo*	לשקול כל דבר לגופו
to know	*ladaat*	לדעת
to reach, obtain	*lehasig*	להשיג
to speak in front of...	*laset dvarim lifney...*	לשאת דברים לפני...
to the best of my ability	*kimeytav yakholti*	כמיטב יכולתי
too, also	*gam*	גם
total darkness	*khoshekh mitsrayim*	חושך מצריים
tremendous, great	*atsum*	עצום
twice	*paamaim*	פעמיים

■ U

ultimately	*besofo shel davar*	בסופו של דבר
unanimous	*pe ekhad*	פה אחד
unbelievable	*lo yeuman*	לא יאומן
understandingly	*bitvuna*	בתבונה
undoubtedly	*barur meal kol safek*	ברור מעל כל ספק
unpleasant	*lo naim*	לא נעים
unsuitable	*lo mat"im*	לא מתאים
until	*ad*	עד
until...	*ad she...; kol od*	עד ש...., כול עוד
until here, this is the limit	*ad kan*	עד כאן
until now	*ad ko*	עד כה

until the end	*ad hasof*	עד הסוף
until then	*ad az*	עד אז
until today	*ad hayom*	עד היום
useless, without benefit	*lelo hoil*	ללא הועיל

■ V

valid	*betokef*	בתוקף
very close connection	*kesher haduk*	קשר הדוק
very good!	*tov meod*	טוב מאוד
very poor level	*tat rama*	תת רמה
vigorously	*bemerets*	במרץ

■ W

Wait a minute!	*rega! daka!*	רגע! דקה!
Want to get together?	*rotse lehipagesh?*	רוצה להפגש?
Want to hear?	*rotse lishmoa?*	רוצה לשמוע?
Want to know what it is about?	*rotse ladaat ma ze?*	רוצה לדעת מה זה?
watch...	*pakakh ain al...*	פקח עין על...
we hope you are right	*nekave she ze nakhon*	נקווה שזה נכון
we shall see	*od nir"e*	עוד נראה
We won't go to the rabbi (well settle this on our own).	*lo nelekh lerav*	לא נלך לרב.
We'll be happy to see you.	*nismakh lir"ot otkha (m), otakh (f)*	נשמח לראות אותך.

we'll meet (again) in...	*nitrae be...*	...נתראה ב
We'll meet afterwards.	*nitrae basof*	נתראה בסוף.
We'll meet again soon.	*nitrae bekarov*	נתראה בקרוב.
we'll meet at...	*nipagesh be...*	...נפגש ב
we'll see	*nir"e*	נראה
we'll wait and see	*nikhye venir"e*	נחיה ונראה
Welcome!	*barukh haba*	ברוך הבא!
well and good	*tov veyafe*	טוב ויפה
What can be done?	*ma efshar laasot?*	מה אפשר לעשות?
What do I care?	*ma ikhpat li?*	מה איכפת לי?
What do you care?	*ma ikhpat lekha?*	מה איכפת לך?
What do you mean "that's the way it is"?!	*ma zot omeret "kakha"?!*	מה זאת אומרת ככה?!
What do you mean "forbidden"?	*ma ze asur?*	מה זה אסור?
What else?	*uma od?*	ומה עוד?
What for?	*leshem ma?*	לשם מה?
What happened?	*ma kara?*	מה קרה?
What is there to talk about?	*al ma yesh ledaber?*	על מה יש לדבר?
What is worth? it's useless?	*ma ze shave?*	מה זה שווה?
What shall we do?	*ma naase?*	מה נעשה?
What would you like?	*ma retsonkha?*	מה רצונך?
What's bothering you?	*ma yesh lekha? lakh (f.)*	מה יש לך?
What's going on here?	*ma holekh kan?*	מה הולך כאן?

What's the difference?	*ma ze meshane?*	?מה זה משנה
What's the matter?	*ma yesh?*	?מה יש
What's this? What's going on?	*ma ze?*	?מה זה
When it's necessary	*kshetsarikh*	כשצריך
when the time comes	*bevo haet*	בבוא העת

Where do you
    hang out?
	*eyfo ata
	    mitrotsets?*
		איפה אתה
		?מתרוצץ

Where have you been?	*eyfo neelamta li?*	?איפה נעלמת לי
Where will you go?	*lean telekh?*	?לאן תלך
while...	*tokh kdey...*	...תוך כדי
while at the same time	*uvo bezman*	ובו בזמן

Who do you think
    you are?
	*lemi ata khoshev
	    et atsmekha?*
		למי אתה חושב
		?את עצמך

Who has arrived?	*mi ze ba?*	?מי זה בא
Who is he anyway?	*mi ze bikhlal?*	?מי זה בכלל
Who wants him?	*mi rotse oto?*	?מי רוצה אותו
Why?	*al shum ma?* *lama?*	?על שום מה ?למה
Why, oh why?	*lama, lama?*	?למה למה

Why are you getting
    excited?
	*ma ata
	    mitragesh?*
		מה אתה
		?מתרגש

Why not?	*lama lo?*	?למה לא
Why should you?	*lama lekha?*	?למה לך
Why so?!	*ma pit"om?!*	!?מה פתאום

with (only) one
    difference
	*behevdel ekhad
	    (bilvad)*
		בהבדל אחד
		(בלבד)

with both hands, with open arms	*beshtey hayadayim*	בשתי הידיים
with love	*mikerev lev*	מקרב לב
with your permission	*birshutkha*	ברשותך
within	*betokh*	בתוך
without any hesistation	*belo tsel shel hisus*	בלא צל של היסוס
without anything	*belo klum*	בלא כלום
without hesitation	*belo hisus*	בלא היסוס
wonder	*pele*	פלא
work horse	*sus avoda*	סוס עבודה

■ Y

Yes, indeed! Correct!	*nakhon meod!*	נכון מאוד!
yes, indeed	*omnam ken*	אמנם כן
yes, of course	*ken, kamuvan*	כן, כמובן
You are forbidden!	*asur lekha! lakh (f.)*	אסור לך!
you can't rely on it	*i-efshar lismokh*	אי אפשר לסמוך
you have no right	*eyn lekha rshut*	אין לך רשות
you never know	*eyn ladaat; i-efshar ladaat*	אין לדעת; אי אפשר לדעת
You see!	*ata roe! at roa!*	אתה רואה! את רואה!
you should know	*ratsui sheteda, she ted"i*	רצוי שתדע (י)

■ Z

| zombi | *golem* | גולם |

Egged (bus company)	*eged*	אגד
coffeehouse	*beyt kafe*	בית קפה
post office	*doar*	דואר
Dan (bus company in Tel Aviv area)	*dan*	דן
grocery	*makolet*	מכולת
taxi	*monit*	מונית
restaurant	*mis"ada*	מסעדה
city center	*merkaz hair*	מרכז העיר
medical clinic	*kupat kholim*	קופת חולים
	mirpaa	מרפאה
Mashbir (major department store chain)	*mashbir*	משביר
police	*mishtara*	משטרה
supermarket	*supermarket*	סופרמרקט
the Israeli army	*tsahal*	צה״ל
taxi service	*shirut*	שירות

- Israel's Hi-Tech and agricultural industries are among the most advanced in the world.
- Israel lists over 100 hi-tech companies on the electronic stock market, Nasdaq, making it the country with the most companies on it, after the United States.
- Israel has 8 high level state universities and many colleges.
- Israel's modern agricultural technology is most known for its innovations in drip-irrigation and desalination methods.
- Israeli drivers are considered a little crazy which might be the result of the hot weather and the dynamic and stressful life of this country.
- The bus is the major form of public transportation in Jerusalem but there is no bus service during the Jewish Sabbath.
- To get from Jerusalem to Tel-Aviv during the week or on the Sabbath, taxis are generally available for about 250 NIS.

Jerusalem - Old City

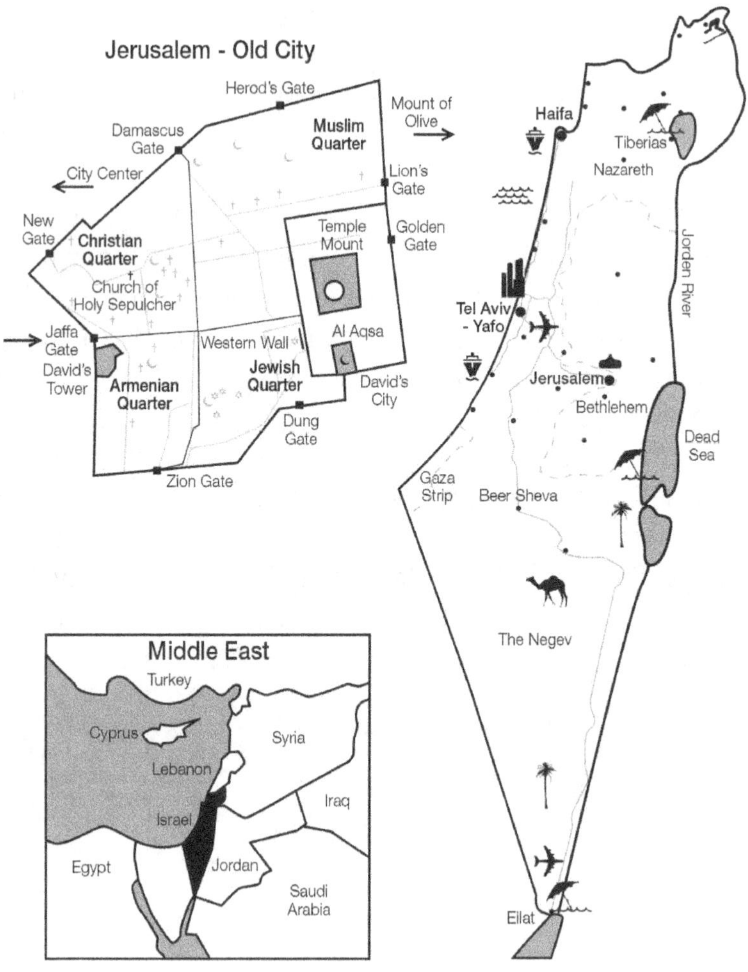

- Ambulance service (Magen David Adom)   101
- Police   100
- Fire Fighters   102
- Information (Bezeq phone directory)   144
- Ben-Gurion International Airport   03-9755555
- Railway service   03-6117000 or *5700
- Taxi service to the Airport from Jerusalem
    02-6253233 or 02-6257227 (Nesher)
- Egged bus service   03-6948888 or *2800
- US consulate – Tel Aviv   03-5197410 or 03-5197575
    – Jerusalem   02-6253258
- British Consulate   02-6935000

Conversion to the Metric system

- 1 meter = 3.28 ft
- 1 kg   = 2.205 lbs

9 798714 765551